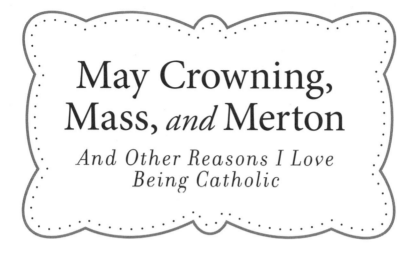

May Crowning, Mass, *and* Merton

And Other Reasons I Love Being Catholic

LIZ KELLY

LOYOLAPRESS.

CHICAGO

D0089576

LOYOLAPRESS.

3441 N. ASHLAND AVENUE
CHICAGO, ILLINOIS 60657
(800) 621-1008
WWW.LOYOLABOOKS.ORG

Unless otherwise noted, the Scripture quotations contained herein are from the New Revised Standard Version Bible: Catholic Edition, copyright © 1993 and 1989 by the Division of Christian Education of the National Council of the Churches of Christ in the U.S.A. Used by permission. All rights reserved.

Catechism quotations are from *Catechism of the Catholic Church,* 2nd ed. (Vatican City: Libreria Editrice Vaticana, 1994).

Adaptation of "Anima Christi" (page 113) used by permission of Byron Hagan.

Fr. Jeff Vonlehmen quotation (pages 161–162) is from *Living Eucharist: The Transforming Presence of Christ* (Liguori, MD: Liguroi Publications, 2002), 31.

Flannery O'Connor quotes in "Flannery O'Connor" (page 66) are taken from *Flannery O'Connor: Spiritual Writings,* unless otherwise noted.

Cover illustration and design by Anni Betts
Art direction by Adam Moroschan
Interior design by Kathryn Seckman

Library of Congress Cataloging-in-Publication Data
Kelly, Liz, 1967-
  May crowning, masses, and Merton : 50 reasons to love being Catholic / Liz Kelly.
    p. cm.
  ISBN 0-8294-2025-8
  1. Catholic Church—Apologetic works. 2. Catholic Church—Doctrines. 3. Catholic Church—Customs and practices. I. Title.
BX1752.K45 2006
282—dc22
                                                2005020940
Printed in the United States of America
06 07 08 09 10 11 12 13 Versa 10 9 8 7 6 5 4 3 2 1

May Crowning, Mass, and Merton

To Anne —
Welcome to the
Church !

Your sponsor,
Orysia Earhart
4-7-07

For my father, Richard

From M-Six

TABLE OF CONTENTS

❸ PART THREE: DEVOTION IN PRACTICE

Acknowledgments

THANK YOU TO ALL MY dear friends who "love me any-way": Mary McCarthy, Pamela Hill, Cristia Lesher, Lil Copan, Sr. Annamarie Stadick, and my brothers and sisters. A special thank-you goes to my mother, Mary, who listened to me read every single word along the way and was encouraging to the last. I appreciate the many hours that you and Dad spent in adoration on this one! To my friends at Loyola, thank you for lending your confidence in me and for sharing your considerable expertise. May God continue to bless the work of your hands. And to Fr. Peter Grover and Fr. Greg and all the priests of the Oblates of the Virgin Mary, thank you for choosing to be priests and for the myriad ways you have ministered to me and to so many others.

Prologue

....

IRONICALLY, WHEN I WAS FORMULATING the topic of reasons to love being Catholic, some of the first things that came to mind were reasons why I did not like being Catholic: guilt, shame, and fear; a pile of negative stereotypes about Catholics that made me feel small, ugly, stupid, close-minded, and weak; and misunderstandings of myself and of the church that led me to leave it for a time.

As I ticked down this list of reasons why I don't like being Catholic—some legitimate, others not—I came up with two basic points of contention.

One: It's hard. Being Catholic has taught me about balance and prudence and the deep joys of daily discipline and commitment, just as training for a triathlon did. But being Catholic is hard. Very hard. It requires all of me. Heaven wants all of me, and every day there are bits and pieces of me that I want to squirrel away for myself, little lusts that I want to indulge, or perhaps pockets of shame or guilt or resentment, or moments of grief or loss I mistakenly believe do not concern God. But heaven still wants all of me—and this is hard. It's both terrifying and relieving to know that once and for all, God wants all of me, just as I am, no adjustments, no tinkering required, no "Well, we want you, but thinner, prettier, holier, more perfect." No, God wants just me right now. Mother Teresa once said that we aim to allow Jesus to use us, just as we are, without our permission. More often than not, the permission I am withholding is out of fear not that God will assign me a task I will hate, but that in seeing me just as I am, with all my faults and deep desires, he will assign me no task at all, will find no use for me.

Two: It's hard. Sometimes it is painful to be Catholic, not because the rules and regulations so often associated with being Catholic are so restrictive, but because the love of heaven leads us to fearless expansiveness, to vast open planes of senses and love so great they cannot be named but only recognized and felt in our deepest weeping core.

As I've filled these pages I have been delighted to unearth a great well of gratitude for the many blessings that being Catholic has poured into my life, my writing, my music, and all my loves. I find in the church as an institution a larger picture of what God has already graciously and most wondrously and efficaciously implanted within me. I feel wildly fortunate that the church is here—one, holy, catholic, and apostolic, established to help support humanity in its quest toward becoming our best selves, the people God intended us to be, his devoted children.

I hope this book will put to rest for some of its readers the misconceptions I have held myself of what it means to be Catholic. I am certain it will not speak to everyone, and that's all right. The journalist Henry Bayard Swope once said, "I cannot give you the formula for success, but I can give you the formula for failure, which is: Try to please everybody." Catholicism is not interested in the success that pleases everybody; instead, I believe it is interested in the success that brings people into loving relationship with God, where we become our best selves. And no matter which way you slice it, that is hard.

Do I have much to learn—of myself, of God, of my church, of you? Oh yes. This is the great joy of it, embracing the mystery, becoming willing to live with questions and to evolve. Am I open to learn? Most days, yes, I hope. Do I wish for greatness, in the sense that it may lead to more learning, deeper understandings that bring greater freedom? Yes.

Dear, sweet Jesus. Let me never settle for *good*. Instead, let me fly, fly, fly toward *greatness*—and find that you are there and have been there, waiting for me all this long, long while. Amen.

PART ONE

Objects with Meaning

The Crucifix

....

I T BEGINS HERE: THE TELLTALE Catholic icon.

My favorite crucifix hangs low over my bed, low enough that I can reach up, take it off its nail, and hold it across my center when I'm in bed meditating or praying or just feeling lonely. It was a gift from my younger brother, something he brought back from a pilgrimage to Medjugorje. It is your standard crucifix: Christ nailed to a tree, the classic pose, the crown of thorns, "INRI" hanging over his head. For many years, it bore the strong aroma of roses—not an uncommon phenomenon for blessed objects brought back from holy places of pilgrimage such as Medjugorje or Fatima—but the scent has faded some. It sits with me now while I write, speaking gently to me and reminding me of our long relationship and the long nights we've kept each other company.

Cradling a crucifix might seem like an odd, or rather fanatical, thing to do, but I like the sense of keeping the cross close to me, close to my heart. I find it comforting, something to hang on to, to grasp when I can't get myself centered or when I feel afraid.

I see a lot of things when I look at my crucifix.

The drawn face of a man abandoned.

Loneliness.

Sorrow.

I see a body with nothing more to give, drained of life, of breath.

I see blood and thorn and nail and nakedness.

Humiliation.

The ruin and wreckage of hatred outpoured.

And pain.

But there are other things to see, too. Even more powerful things.

I see understanding and compassion. No matter how low I feel, I see that I am understood, and I am not alone.

I see gentleness, and honesty, innocence, authenticity.

I see not the absence of strength, but the presence of surrender.

I see a distinct lack of self-pity.

Sometimes when I look at the crucifix, I see other people: a former boss who was greatly and unfairly burdened, a dear friend who suffers from a chronic and unpredictable illness, an addict I met on a train ride, a coworker abandoned by a husband, a man who struggles with paranoid schizophrenia and with the side effects of his drug treatments. And I remember to pray for others and their suffering and, as much as I am able, to be a catalyst to alleviate the suffering around me, to move through life as a healing balm.

When I look at the crucifix, I also see a promise kept. God said he would love me, know me, and never abandon me, no matter what, no matter the cost. He keeps his word.

To some degree, the Christian life begins with the Crucifixion. It is the gateway to everything else. Accepting the Crucifixion is the first step toward trusting that with Jesus, to die is to rise again. Accepting the Crucifixion is agreeing with your whole person that you want to at least become willing to give your whole life for love. We are reminded of this sacrifice by the crucifixes we hang over our beds, around our necks, from our rearview mirrors, in our churches, and on our walls—the myriad ways we plant them throughout our daily worlds.

But that's just a place to start. The Good News is that it doesn't end there.

2

Holy Water, Incense, and Candles

T HEY ARE SACRAMENTALS, PHYSICAL SIGNS or reminders of the seven sacraments. They are surely one of my
favorite traditions within the church. Sacramentals take
the spiritual graces of God and bring them to our senses
and experience in a way that heightens and strengthens our
understanding of the glory, majesty, and holiness of God,
along with his great love to extend himself to us through
the sacraments.

Sacramentals speak to the larger picture. The seven
sacraments—baptism, reconciliation, holy communion,
confirmation, matrimony, holy orders, and anointing of
the sick—are outward signs of inward grace given to us by
Jesus. The church teaches that "sacramentals do not confer
the grace of the Holy Spirit in the way that the sacraments
do, but by the Church's prayer, they prepare us to receive
grace and dispose us to cooperate with it" (*Catechism*,
1670). Catholics "cooperate" with heaven when we dab
our foreheads with holy water, burn incense, and light

candles. We perform these small outward signs as a means of demonstrating an interior that is soft to the work of heaven through the Holy Spirit.

Holy Water

I will sprinkle clean water upon you,
and you shall be clean from all your
uncleannesses.
—Ezekiel 36:25

A dear friend with virtually no experience of any religion—a devout "cynicist," as he calls himself—recently came to noon Mass with me. He saw me dip my fingers in the holy water stoup outside the sanctuary doors before entering and promptly stopped me as I was making the sign of the cross. "All right, before we go any further," he said, "what is *up* with the holy water bit?"

Well, that's one way to put the question.

Holy water is meant to remind us of our baptism. Usually holy water is simply plain water that has been blessed by a priest. A touch of salt is added because it is a preservative, and holy water is meant to "preserve us" from sin.

It was as Jesus was rising out of the water following his baptism that the clouds opened and the spirit of God descended upon him, and "a voice from heaven said, 'This is my Son, the Beloved, with whom I am well pleased'" (Matthew 3:17). When I bless myself with holy water upon entering the church, not only am I beginning to prepare myself for Mass and for prayer, but also I may recall this scene from the Gospel and remember, "So too am I beloved. Oh Jesus, help me be pleasing to the Father, as you are."

Holy water works as a tiny drop of a reminder that I have been baptized and, in that, appointed, blessed, and anointed for my role on the planet. Christ was baptized and then entered into his public ministry, performing his first miracle at the wedding feast of Cana, turning water into wine. So too have I been chosen, baptized, and prepared. So too am I to go forward and enter into the world to fulfill my vocation.

When we dip our fingers in water and make the sign of the cross, damp and blessed on our body, it is a deep reminder of all these things.

Incense

My favorite church in Boston is St. Clement Eucharistic Shrine. It is run by the Oblates of the Virgin Mary, a lovely order of beautiful priests whose seminary sits next door to the shrine. I introduced a close friend to it not long ago. Upon entering the sanctuary, she took a deep breath, exhaled, and said, "It smells like Jesus in here."

I love the smell of "church," the waft of incense that has worked its way into the very walls. It is comforting and reminds me of liturgy at its warmest, finest, and most ceremonious: midnight Mass, Easter Vigil, adoration. The psalmist says, "Let my prayer be counted as incense before you, / and the lifting up of my hands as an evening sacrifice" (Psalm 141:2). And Proverbs remembers that "perfume and incense make the heart glad" (27:9). In Revelation, "the smoke of the incense, with the prayers of the saints, rose before God from the hand of the angel" (8:4).

Have you ever wondered why God bothered with smell? There has to be more to it than keeping us from eating something rancid or knowing when to change the baby's diaper, though those are certainly productive uses of our olfactory nerve.

Smelling is an unconscious, innate activity. Some researchers believe that our sense of smell may have been one of the most important to possess for survival; in primitive times it would have been a tremendous advantage to smell prey or predator before seeing it. Tied to the limbic system of the brain, which registers emotions such as pleasure, fear, and pain, our sense of smell can have a very powerful impact on our mood and can immediately and unconsciously stir up deep memories.

The history of incense is equally complex and tied to our earliest forms of prayer and meditation. From ancient times and our first interaction with fire, we discovered that certain substances produced very pleasing aromas. Because of the intricate way that smell affects us mentally and emotionally, it probably wasn't long before we discovered that certain aromas helped to produce various effects: calming scents to prepare us for prayer, meditation, and contemplation, or stimulating scents for rites of celebration and healing. Additionally, certain substances, such as frankincense, were costly. To burn them liberally, releasing their pleasing aroma, was considered a generous offering to God.

The church continues to use incense in practical and symbolic ways: to prepare the faithful for ceremony, prayer, or adoration; to offer our prayers and works to God; to bless holy objects, the altar, the congregation, and the bread and wine; and to bless funeral and other processions. The use of incense in church may also help to stir our collective memory, calling to mind a number of moving symbols: prayers rising to heaven, the cloud in which God appeared to the Israelites to lead them through the desert. It is a reminder of the Holy Spirit that descended upon the Virgin Mary and upon the apostles at Pentecost, every Catholic at his or her confirmation, and the same Holy Spirit that descends upon the water and wine at Mass during the transubstantiation.

Lord, may my life be an offering of sweet incense rising to make your heart glad.

Candles

Candles have dozens of uses within the church. One of the most popular and most frequently associated with Catholicism is the use of the votive. The name "votive" comes from the Latin *votum*, which means "vow." It is very common to see little villages of votive candles, often at the back of church or on either side of the sanctuary, gathered at the foot of a statue of one of the saints or of Jesus or Mary. When Catholics say to you, "I'll light a candle for you," they mean that they will say a prayer for you, possibly requesting the intercession of one of the saints. They light a candle for you to recognize that prayer or to say thank you for a prayer answered.

There is the tabernacle or sanctuary lamp—another candle—placed near the tabernacle where the Eucharist is housed, signifying the living presence of God. We have candles specifically designated for Easter, Christmas, baptisms, marriage, and other sacraments or holy days. Our family used Advent candles in an Advent wreath every year; there are typically three purple and one pink candle representing the weeks of preparation of Advent. Lighting the advent candle before meals was a means of gathering us together to recognize and celebrate the holy season.

Even as I sit here, I have a candle burning. It is my little petition to the Holy Spirit to come and light my way, to burn through me to reach the page, as corny as that sounds. It helps. I don't think heaven needs my burning candle any more than it needs holy water or incense. Sacramentals are for us, because we are sensory beings, and symbolism and sacramentals help infuse the spiritual into the other planes of our experience—physical, emotional, mental. We light our candles to remind us that Jesus is the "light of the world" (John 8:12) and that "God is light and in him there is no darkness at all" (1 John 1:5). Amen.

3

HOLY GEAR

....

WE CATHOLICS LIKE OUR ATTIRE. Our babies have their baptismal gowns; our altar servers their robes; our priests their vestments; our brides their white wedding dresses; our communicants their veils; and some of our children, their Catholic school uniforms. These articles of clothing speak of roles and preparation; they speak of unity and uniqueness; they reflect on the outside the way we are feeling on the inside, and they share our faith with the world in a wonderfully colorful and open way. They remind us of who we are and who we hope to be; they cloak and cover; they expose and identify. Ultimately, they symbolize and magnify the riches of tradition and the importance of the various roles and rites of passage in the life of faith.

First Communion Dresses

Mine was pink. And, as was all my clothing until I was about twenty years old, my first Holy Communion dress was a hand-me-down. I still remember how cool the satin sheath felt against my skin; covered in white lace, it slipped over me like an onionskin.

In the picture from my first Holy Communion, I am walking down the aisle of the church of my childhood, St. Raphael's. My hands are folded, my white kneesocks pulled up snug to my kneecaps, my white sandals strapped on tight, a long white veil draped over my light brown hair. The camera snapped just as my eyes blinked shut; I look so peaceful, so serene with my eyes closed that you'd think I was sleepwalking. But I was most alert. I will not forget the significance of that day, the day I was invited by God himself to be the bride.

We don't dress up our children like brides and grooms for their first Holy Communion because we think it's charming, though it may be. The clothing is a reflection of the greater relationship forming between Christ and the communicant. Bridegroom and bride. We are chosen, prepared, and called forth for initiation into a holy communion with God, a body-and-blood relationship that will bring forth life in all our relationships. In these ways, Holy Communion reminds us of wedding vows and speaks to the part of us that longs to be chosen.

Wedding Dresses

When I was in Rome, one of the most moving ceremonies I got to observe at St. Peter's Basilica was the blessing of marriages by the pope. Hundreds of couples gathered on the steps of the cathedral and were seated in hard plastic chairs flanking the pontiff. It was a sea of black and white, with many of the couples dressed in rented gowns and tuxedos for the occasion. Each couple approached the pope, knelt before him, and received his blessing. In some cases, especially with older couples who had clearly been married a long time, the pope would hover over a couple a bit longer, perhaps touching the face of the bride or placing his hand on the head of the groom.

That so many of these couples went to the trouble of putting on wedding attire, even though some of them had traveled from other countries to receive the papal blessing, speaks to the significance of preparing ourselves, of wearing on the outside the roles we live out on the inside. Dressing for one's wedding is certainly not a tradition that belongs solely to the Catholic Church. Instead, it is one of the many ways that the church intertwines with the world around her.

Wedding attire is also an outward expression that mirrors the dignity of the sacrament. The special attention we give to our appearance is merely an outward way of saying, "What happens between this man and this woman is sacramental."

Vestments

After nearly thirty years of working as an attorney, my father became a judge. I first saw him in his judge's robe when he was being sworn in, and this moment stuck with me. The symbolism of his robe was powerful. It spoke to his authority and the responsibility that went with it. His robe was a reminder to all in the courtroom that it was his job to interpret and apply the law with reason, understanding, honor, and, ultimately, fairness. His robe said that he was willing to take on the burden of deciding the fate of abused children, drunken drivers, and delinquents headed down the wrong road. It could not have been easy.

I was reminded of my father's swearing-in when a seminarian at my church recently took his first vows of chastity, poverty, and obedience. This beautiful young man knelt before the seminary director and proclaimed his intentions to become a priest. While we sang songs of thanksgiving, he was led to a room at the side of the sanctuary, and moments later he emerged in his first cassock. It was stirring to observe this exterior representation of the interior journey to love and serve God with a singleness of purpose. It was his outward demonstration of an inner acceptance of the responsibility that comes with becoming a priest.

Priestly vestments act in a similar manner and greatly enrich the experience of the Mass for me. They are visual reminders to those of us at services that the priest has been especially prepared for his role at the altar and that his calling is different from ours in the pews. The two most distinct pieces to priestly vestments are the alb and the chasuble. The alb is the white linen robe worn underneath the more colorful chasuble and is a symbol of purity and innocence. The chasuble is generally one of four colors: red, white, violet, or green. Red is worn on the feast days that remember the martyred saints who shed their blood for their faith. It is also the color of fire and is worn on feast days, such as Pentecost, that honor the Holy Spirit. White is a symbol of glory or innocence or purity and is used on various feast days of our Lady, angels, and saints who were not martyred. Violet is worn during the seasons of preparation, Lent and Advent, and is also a symbol of penance. Green, symbolic of hope and growth of the church, is worn at various times throughout the year.

I love that God bothered with color and with hearts and imaginations that would crave ceremony. The holy gear that marks the life of Catholics also reminds me that my world is a colorful world, not just black and white and gray. Similarly, my faith will have shades and colors, responsibilities and accountabilities, honors and duties, and many beautiful seasons to be lived, embraced, and celebrated.

4

The Rosary

....

Rosaries have worked their way into my purse, my gym bag, my luggage, my computer case, my desk at work. They hang off my bedpost, sit in a tangle on my dresser, and have settled into countless drawers—just as they have settled into the very creases and crevices of my soul's skin. My little anchors. And of course, they're not just mine. As I was walking down the street a few days ago, a big, burly guy drove by in a big, burly vehicle with a rosary hanging from the rearview mirror. I smiled and thought to myself, *Dude, I know exactly how you feel.*

What *is* the appeal?

The rosary has been called "the epitome of the Gospel." Evolving over centuries, it has become—for Catholics as well as non-Catholics—an effective and popular means for meditating primarily on the life of Jesus. The rosary invites the person praying to contemplate the most significant moments of Jesus' life, death, and resurrection and is composed of the most common Catholic prayers, including the Apostles' Creed, the Our Father, the Hail Mary, and the Glory Be. The physical rosary is made of five sections of stringed beads, which serve as tallying devices for the prayers. The person praying names a "mystery" on each section to facilitate meditation on events from the life of Christ, such as the birth of Jesus, the Transfiguration, the Crucifixion, and the Resurrection. The rosary is a simple yet effective means for anyone at any level of experience to begin the practice of meditation and draw closer to Jesus. I owe a great debt to this simple devotion; it is not an exaggeration to say that it saved my life.

My first experiences of the rosary involved praying it with my family on Christmas Eve. Indeed, it is a popular family prayer because of its simplicity and repetition. As an adult, I returned to rosary meditation during an especially tumultuous time because of this simplicity. In my emotional struggles, I found the repetition comforting; it cleared my head and heart in much the same manner that going for a long run or listening to the ocean would, only the effects were much, much deeper and longer lasting. It was gentle and easy and led me to profounder meditation and contemplation, which would eventually bring about great healing on every level. (This story can be found in my book *The Rosary: A Path into Prayer.*)

The rosary is largely considered a Marian devotion, but it should be noted that Jesus is the focus of the meditation. The Our Father prayer is taken directly from the lips of Christ and takes an appropriate place at the head of each decade (a group of ten Hail Marys). The Hail Mary, the prayer most often repeated in the rosary, continues the rosary's absolutely Christocentric focus; the name of Jesus is not only the physical median of the prayer, but also the spiritual centerpiece of all Marian devotion. Without Jesus, there is no Marian devotion.

In brief, the Hail Mary is drawn largely from the Gospel of Luke. In the Gospel, the angel Gabriel visits Mary and addresses her in this manner: "Hail Mary, full of grace, the Lord is with you." Gabriel goes on to reveal to Mary that she will become pregnant by the Holy Spirit and give birth to Jesus. This angelic salutation—called the Annunciation—marks Jesus' entrance into human history. The saving work of the Father was brought about when Mary responded, "Let it be with me according to your word." The prayer continues with another passage from the Gospel of Luke, where Mary's cousin Elizabeth tells her, "Blessed are you among women, and blessed is the fruit of your womb." (For more on the development of the Hail Mary, see chapter 26, "The 'Ave Maria'.")

The prayer concludes with a simple petition: "Holy Mary, Mother of God, pray for us sinners, now and at the hour of our death." We ask Mary to pray for us because her unique role as the mother of Jesus, the mother of God, also makes her a powerful intercessor. Catholics turn to her often, but this devotion is not to be confused with worship.

The rosary was used throughout the history of the church as a means to teach the life of Jesus to audiences who either lacked access to books or could not read. The rosary was also a method of drawing believers into communal prayer and greater fellowship.

While rosary meditation is entirely optional for Catholics, its practice has been strongly encouraged by many prominent figures within the church, including Pope John Paul II and many of the saints. The church teaches that

> meditation engages thought, imagination, emotion, and desire. This mobilization of faculties is necessary in order to deepen our convictions of faith, prompt the conversion of our heart, and strengthen our will to follow Christ. Christian prayer tries above all to meditate on the mysteries of Christ, as in *lectio divina* or the rosary. This form of prayerful reflection is of great value, but Christian prayer should go further: to the knowledge of the love of the Lord Jesus, to union with him. (*Catechism,* 2708)

The explanation or study of rosary devotion could never replace the actual practice of it. I began slowly, with a decade now and then, and was drawn more deeply into my faith life. I have grown to love my rosaries and feel the need to always have them close by, if not on my person.

They remind me of my momma in heaven, that magnificent woman in the sky, always interceding for me, loving me home to heaven. The beads sound good jangling in my pocket or thumping gently against my chest when I go running. I don't have to be praying a rosary—just as I don't have to be at Mass or adoration—to feel the presence, strength, comfort, power, life, virtue, and mystery of all that these beads embody.

5

Kneelers

....

I CONFESS I AM THE kind of person who really likes to throw her whole body into things. For example, I like to go to adoration late at night when no one else is around and fall flat on my face before God. Sometimes it is an action of surrender; at other times, fatigue; at still others, penitence or all-out supplication. I have also developed a habit of surrendering to God "face up." Rather than burying my face in the carpet, I will lie on my back, arms outstretched, and await whatever God may have for me to take up, embrace whatever graces or challenges he may wish to give me. Whatever my posture, I never want to do anything with just my head, just my heart, or just my body. My prayer posture has the potential to unite my body, mind, and spirit, which makes the experience more meaningful, not for God but for me.

For this reason, I love kneelers.

They are falling out of fashion, I know. Some people want to remove them from churches entirely, and they may have valid reasons for wanting to do so. But I would miss them. I once heard that camels are great practitioners of surrender because they start and end each day on their knees. We could learn something from the great, hairy dromedary, and I keep a little camel statue in my office to remind me of this throughout the day. Perhaps if I were humbler, less self-involved, then maybe I wouldn't need to be reminded to surrender, and maybe I wouldn't need to kneel in church—or elsewhere—to show my respect and reverence in this way. But I do.

I believe that God wants the whole person. Whether in church or at the side of the bed in the morning, kneeling is one small way we can say, "Here, Father, take all of me; even my body longs to serve you." And when we're not so anxious to love and serve God, kneeling can be a reminder to us of who we are and who God is. Sometimes by first disciplining our body, our heart and mind follow.

We kneel for a lot of reasons: to say thank you; to say, "I acknowledge you in your holy inhabitance"; to plead for mercy; to ask for help; to focus our energy on something greater than ourselves; to show respect; to appropriately lower ourselves before the Almighty. We think it's adorable when a man proposes to a woman "on bended knee," but to show such devotion to God is becoming passé. We want God to be our buddy—and make no mistake, God is deeply devoted to friendship with us—but God is also our creator, and that requires respect.

This is why people ascend the Scala Santa in Rome on their knees; it's why they go up the asphalt trail to the apparition chapel at Fátima on their knees. When my brother, a teenager at the time, came home from a pilgrimage to Fátima, he had holes in the knees of his jeans, and they were stained with blood. I am moved every time I think of him processing forward on his knees, anonymous among so many other pilgrims on their knees but far from anonymous to God. How moved heaven must have been to see his earnest expression of devotion, supplication, and homage.

A man I know who wants to have kneelers removed from our church tells me that the earliest Masses were never said in churches and never involved kneeling. He tells me that standing during various points of the Mass was actually a greater sign of respect and reverence in the early church. Maybe this is true, but as the Mass has evolved since the Last Supper in its appointments and particulars, the meaning of the Mass, and the sacrifice we celebrate there, have not. I cannot help but think that our church culture, as well as our society at large, is moving into precarious territory when we start talking about removing kneelers from the sanctuary. We need to be clear as to why we would recommend such an action.

Kneeling admits to a need—the need for God. As a culture, we seem to be in a desperate race to rid ourselves of this need for something greater than ourselves, and if that is not an act of arrogance, it is at least an act absent of humility. What I have come to believe is that our need for God does not makes us weak; it makes us fully human. There is great power in recognizing the difference.

The spiritual posture of one's heart is greatly reflected in the physical posture of one's body. If there are times when I can kneel before my Creator, Ecclesiastes assures me that there are times when I will dance before him as well. Or maybe I feel moved to surrender facedown. Perhaps I am in a place and space with God where I feel him calling me to surrender "face up"; by all means, I must follow the leaning of my spirit. And if I feel moved to kneel, then there surely must be blessing in that posture too.

In this day of war, terror, deprivation, selfishness, and cruelty without equal, surely there is cause to kneel. The sorrows and fears of our world bring into sharp relief our great disdain for one another and for life. Maybe it is too great a leap to suggest so, but I believe that the crusty old kneeler in our struggling church just may be the tool we need to help us find our way back to holiness and virtue— the very holy and abundant order of things in which there is room enough for all of God's creatures to flourish.

6

THE *PIETÀ*

....

For God so loved the world . . .
—John 3:16

WHEN I WAS IN ROME volunteering during the Jubilee, I was assigned one day to stand in front of Michelangelo's *Pietà* in a bright blue poncho and make myself available to any wandering pilgrim who might need my help. It was an enviable post, there in front of what might be one of the world's most famous works of art, completed by a man just twenty-four years old and capturing with matchless craft and beauty this devastating, intimate moment between mother and Son. The crucified Christ in the arms of his mother.

Standing there for six hours, I had abundant time to absorb the work and to collect the comments of others as they experienced it—many, like me, for the first time in person. *It's so big. It's so real. It's so moving. It's so sad.* Sometimes they would ask me to take their picture in front of it, and their smiles were not the broad smiles of tourists on vacation, but soft and pensive at the grief unveiled behind them. Situated just inside and to the right of the main entrance to St. Peter's Basilica, the *Pietà* is often one of the first things that visitors notice. This particular spot was an interesting choice for the work, because the entrance to St. Peter's is a fairly bustling place when tourists and pilgrims are about. However, the air becomes suddenly more somber and still when you stand in front of this work. Even the voices of tour guides seem to lower and soften when they explain that Michelangelo was angry when he overheard people attributing the work to another artist. He was so angry, in fact, that he sneaked back in at night to sign his name to Mary's sash, and later so regretted his outburst that he vowed he would never sign another work of his again.

Mother and Son. A reverse prodigal of sorts. In his wonderful book *The Return of the Prodigal Son,* Henri Nouwen writes, "The finding has the losing in the background, the returning has the leaving under its cloak. Looking at the tender and joy-filled return, I have to dare to taste the sorrowful events that preceded it." Similarly, but in reverse, the Pietà asks us to taste death and the grief of innocent blood shed, but hiding under the cloak of betrayal and sorrow is the promise of resurrection and hope for new life.

At times, I wonder at heaven and the order of things. Is it better or necessary somehow to have the dying first and the resurrection later? Why is the Pietà the icon that endures? Must we have the dying at all?

We all have our own Pietà moments, some so much like the real thing that we can hardly bear them. In his tender book, *A Grief Unveiled,* author Gregory Floyd exposes his family's grieving process following the death of his seven-year-old son in an accident. Upon learning that their son Johnny had died, Floyd and his wife, Maureen, were faced with the bittersweet choice of whether to donate his young organs. Floyd unveils one of the most excruciating moments when, after his son's organs were harvested, Floyd and his wife were each allowed to hold their child one final time. He writes:

Some moments are so sacred that one dare not clothe them in anything but silence. I watched as Maureen held her dead child in her arms, and listened as she drew her child to her breast and touched his face with hers. "John-Paul, it was such a privilege to be your mother. I love you so much. I'm so sorry this happened. Pray for us." It was my turn. I wept and wept. There was something urgent about wanting to hold in death this flesh I loved so much in life. There were no words to describe the pain. It was unimaginable, inconceivable, untouchable. I had always thought that the death of a child was the greatest cross a parent could be asked to bear. And here we were, staggering under its weight.

There is no easy answer, no ready response to this picture; however, Floyd's work points brilliantly to the mysterious consolation that even God grieves. The Father is in fact a bereaved parent too, "and therein [lies] my hope," writes Floyd. Indeed, the Father is grieving at the loss of his Son and of all his children who have turned their faces away from him, whose love has been lost to the world through sin, pride, addiction, unbelief, hardness of heart.

In our own Pietà moments, can we look to the beauty of mother and Son and take consolation, even direction? Can we find acceptance in the composition, see perfection and grace in the lines? Looking beneath the cloak of grief and death, do we find hope, resurrection, eternal life?

I learned much about the *Pietà* that day at St. Peter's, about the genius of Michelangelo's portrayal of the human body; about the man who once leaped onto it, attacking the sculpture and taking off a part of Christ's foot, which was later restored; about the composition and the unusual choice of the artist to portray Mary so young.

Curiously, it was the children who stood in front of the *Pietà* who posed the most enigmatic questions.

"Mommy, is he sick?"

"No, honey, that's Jesus, and he died."

"Why did he die, Mamma?"

That is the question, isn't it? Out of the mouths of babes.

7

MICHELANGELO'S CREATION FRESCOES
IN THE SISTINE CHAPEL

....

I FIRST BECAME ACQUAINTED WITH the name Michelangelo when I was about nine years old. One of my early vocational inclinations was to be a painter. My mother, in encouraging this notion, gave me a book on art that presented overviews of major movements, including the Renaissance. Not knowing what the word meant, I promptly looked it up in my dictionary and came upon the expression "Renaissance man." The names listed as examples included the usual suspects: Michelangelo Buonarroti, Leonardo da Vinci, Sir Walter Raleigh. But I was captivated by the definition, which I remember to this day: "one who masters multiple disciplines such as science, art, and literature." I thought with delight, *Who knew this was an option?* Now I wouldn't have to pick and choose between painter, astronaut, writer, Olympic gymnast, and equestrian. In that nine-year-old moment when anything was possible and the world was mine, I decided that I would be a "Renaissance woman."

Funny how things look so much less exhausting at nine than they do at thirty-seven.

Many years passed from the time of my nine-year-old declaration to when I met Michelangelo's work in person in the Sistine Chapel in Rome. I liken my experience upon entering the chapel to traveling through Alaska. You can read about Alaska in books all you like and you can study it in classrooms, but until you actually set foot on the spongy tundra you really have no idea what all the fuss is about. The experience of entering the chapel, viewing the immensity of the works, and smelling the faint aroma of incense that has bled its way into the walls over hundreds of years of Masses could not be replaced by a gift shop poster or a textbook description.

God has long used artists to raise our thoughts to contemplation of holy, inspired truths and our hearts to greater sanctity. The Sistine Chapel, whose frescoes illustrate through their stories the primary tenets of the faith, from creation to the final judgment, provides an extraordinary opportunity for inspiration and greater understanding of theology, art, and, ultimately, God's love for his most precious creation, his sons and daughters.

Though the entire Sistine Chapel is masterful, the creation frescoes on the ceiling are my favorite works and some of its most famous. I saw them after they had undergone a major restoration, which was completed in 1994. Michelangelo's depiction of Genesis begins with the swirling and powerful figure of God appointing night and day, sun and moon, planets, stars, and vegetation. The artist portrays the all-powerful God of creation as fierce and focused. Creation in this Renaissance world is a thunderous, almost violent act set into motion by a God whose strength roars yet is wielded with perfect poise. To the sun and the moon, he is commanding and stern, and they can only obey and be as they are appointed. But to the reclining Adam, God extends his gentle touch, meeting Adam's gaze as he does so. A still more subdued and approachable heavenly Father draws out daughter Eve with an even gentler beckoning to be.

It is a curious help that one has to stand beneath the works and turn one's head up to view them properly (for though you may try, the guards will not allow you to lie on the floor). This posture in itself magnifies the grandeur of the act of creation and the vast and matchless power of the Creator. It is interesting that the Hebrew verb for "create," *bara,* always has God for its subject; indeed, there is only one Creator who "in the beginning . . . created the heavens and the earth" from nothing.

The church teaches that "the truth about creation is so important for all of human life that God in his tenderness wanted to reveal to his People everything that is salutary to know on the subject. . . . Creation is . . . the first and universal witness to God's all-powerful love" (*Catechism,* 287–88). Life is a gift, God's most loving gift. Our origin, our genesis as living, breathing, thinking, feeling beings, is in God, the almighty one, the creator. We, his creatures, remain entirely dependent upon and sustained by him, whether or not we recognize it.

It is precisely under the frescoes detailing creation that our cardinals gather to elect popes. In Pope John Paul II's homily at the Mass celebrating the completion of the restoration, he said, "The truths of our faith speak to us here from all sides." Thus, it is a most fitting and sacred space in which to await the inspiration of the Holy Spirit to guide and direct the church in appointing her leadership.

The pope went on to say that "the Sistine Chapel is precisely—if one may say so—the sanctuary of the theology of the human body. In witnessing to the beauty of man created by God as male and female, it also expresses in a certain way, the hope of a world transfigured, the world inaugurated by the Risen Christ." In this powerful God appointing the heavens, I can trust too that I have been created for a purpose, a heavenly appointment. We have all been created with "an appointment" in the heart and mind of heaven. The God of all creation has work for me to do. How magnificent that he has given me more power than the sun, for the sun has no choice in accepting its appointment, but I do.

In this way, the creation frescoes remind us that, as with Adam, it is the touch of God that brings us life. As with Eve, it is his gentle beckoning that will draw us into the life for which we have been designed. It is the sacrificial love of Jesus that brings us rebirth and eternal life, our spiritual renaissance. Like these frescoes, we need restoration, that gentle, slow, delicate touch-up from God to help us remain luminous and beautiful, true to our original nature.

Maybe I won't get to be a gymnast or an astronaut, but in his gentle way, Jesus has led me to become that Renaissance woman I so longed to be as a child. He has offered me spiritual renewal and rebirth, and there can be no more important embodiment of "renaissance" than that.

8

THE SCALA SANTA AND DEVOTION

It is one of my favorite pilgrimage spots of all time: la Scala Santa, the Holy Steps. They are the twenty-eight steps that led up to the court of Pontius Pilate, which Jesus ascended and descended on the day of his trial and judgment. Tradition holds that Constantine's mother, St. Helena, was a fervid collector of relics and brought the steps to Rome from the Holy Land around AD 326. Up and down, Christ walked these steps, bleeding on the marble now covered with wood. Pilgrims ascend the steps on their knees, occasionally pausing to bend over and kiss the spots where the bloodstains of Jesus, now dark with age, are encased in glass. The steps are located across the street from San Giovanni in Laterano in Rome. Once I discovered them, I was hooked on the devotion, ascending the steps nearly every day while working as a volunteer during the Jubilee Year.

Rome is filled to capacity with relics of every kind. Whether you believe they are real or not, they are meant to help the faithful, to serve as vehicles of greater hope and greater faith. Devotional practices such as climbing the Holy Steps are central to my experience as a Catholic. Maybe you think this kind of devotion is hokey; I used to. But I don't think God would dismiss any act, any offering, or any gift, no matter how minor or ridiculous, when offered with love.

Devotion, according to Webster's is "love given with the whole heart and will." When I was twelve, I took a babysitting class, and one of the teachers told us something I will never forget. She said that if a child ever offered us a gift, any gift, even if it was a macaroni necklace or a mud duck, we should always accept it as a treasure. To reject it for any reason would be a crushing experience for the child. I had a younger brother, and it made me shudder to think of making fun of something he had given me as a gift, so I understood the teacher completely. To reject a gift from a child would be most unloving, and the child would interpret it as a rejection of him- or herself.

I think of this in relation to my devotion to my heavenly Father. We come to God with our spiritual mud ducks, with our rosaries and prayers like necklaces made from macaroni, with the pilgrimages we make and the candles we light, and, like the eternal Father that he is, God delights in them. He accepts them with the same level of devotion with which they were offered. A father never rejects the gift of his child offered in love.

Devotion is a life stance, a lifestyle, fed by *love*.

When I returned to the United States from Rome, I moved to New Hampshire. Eight miles from my front door was another set of Holy Steps, at the Shrine of Our Lady of La Salette, overlooking Lake Mascoma. I would sometimes ride my bike there and walk through the rosary garden or the outdoor stations of the cross. The holy steps at La Salette were decidedly not St. Helen's Holy Steps, but rather a wooden replica painted an antique blue, with a large sculpted crucifix set at the top, where the steps ascended into a wooded hillside. And I would ascend those steps too, just as I had the ones in Rome, carrying my petitions and thanksgivings, carrying my supplication, wearing my devotion in my knees.

Do I believe my mud-duck devotions change anything in heaven? I don't know, but I believe that my Father accepts them with delight. This changes me. And that is miracle enough.

9

Wedding Bands
on the Hands of Nuns

In order to understand my affinity for wedding bands on the hands of nuns, it might be helpful to first understand some of the history behind the traditional marriage symbol.

The earliest record of women wearing wedding bands dates back thousands of years. The ancient Egyptians believed that the vein in the third finger on the left hand ran straight to the heart. Called the *vena amoris* in Latin, this vein, they believed, was tied to a supernatural love. They would wrap a reed around the finger, believing that this "circle with no end" tapped into divine love. Over the centuries, iron replaced reeds, and then gold and other precious metals replaced iron. The Puritans, who thought jewelry too frivolous and showy, exchanged the very practical if unromantic wedding thimble. During World War II, when soldiers faced months and even years of separation from their wives, men, too, began to wear rings, as a reminder of the beloved who awaited their safe return.

The wedding band has had darker associations as well; it was a sign in Roman times that a woman was a man's property. Ouch. But even a good tradition can be bastardized. This painful reminder of our tendency to devalue one another should not be dismissed, but I don't want to dwell on it either.

I used to think that those who chose religious life were missing out, making a huge and wholly unnecessary sacrifice that would leave their lives lacking and disconnected. This immature thinking was likely the product of not only a culture obsessed with romantic love to the point where little else even exists, but also my misunderstanding regarding the nature of married life and religious life, and the meaning of vocation and consecrated life. I was convinced there could be no satisfaction outside of romantic love.

One of the first wedding bands I can recall being worn by a nun was that of my high school art teacher, Sr. DeLourdes. She was about four feet tall and possessed a sprightly quality. Her hands would shadow mine as I practiced my calligraphy or drawing, so they were frequently in the forefront of my world, and I remember them, wrinkled and old, with their protruding veins and age spots, gentle and warm and quick to offer correction and guidance on my canvases. As my hands age, I see hers more and more in my own.

She was the first to explain to me that she was in fact "taken," married, a bride of Christ, as it were. I had imagined her life to be somewhat lonely or isolated, certainly lacking because she had no husband to go home to. My house was filled with siblings and parents and various dogs and birds and guinea pigs. What did Sr. DeLourdes have?

I had a very tight definition of family and marriage, and I couldn't imagine finding fullness and satisfaction outside of it. In fact, I had no concept of "vocation" beyond marriage and family. Still, like many young girls, I occasionally felt a tug toward religious life as a nun. I still do on occasion, particularly as my life draws forward and I remain single, yet desire community.

I don't mean to suggest that those who lead the single life but do not wear rings do not have ties to supernatural love. Love between the religious and God mimics marriage, which is why Christ compares his relationship with the church to a marriage relationship. Sr. DeLourdes's ring simply gave me a deeper appreciation for the sweetness of her choice. What I once saw as lonely or lacking now had greater fullness and a consummation. The only consummation our culture tends to honor or acknowledge is that of the senses. Hers was of the soul. And that was lovely to behold and just as concrete.

Her Beloved awaited her safe return to heaven with no less passion and depth than anyone who awaits the return of a soldier called to battle. And that's what her ring reminds me of still: that our heavenly Beloved, mine and yours, waits for us, longs for us, and is united to us with a supernatural *vena amoris*, that vein carrying our lifeblood straight to the heart of God.

When nuns wear wedding bands, they remind us that religious life is equally important and tied to that supernatural love without end.

PART TWO

Those Who Journey with Us

10

MARY

·················

ON A RECENT WRITER'S RETREAT led by Vinita Wright, I was given an exercise called "The Journey." The exercise consisted of envisioning a door, behind which our "creative gifts would find their place and flourish." The door was a three days' journey away. The assignment was to tell the story of those three days.

As I began the exercise, I could not envision a door but sensed instead a precipice of some kind, high atop a mountain draped in heavy fog. I could not see the precipice, but I felt it there, hidden in the dense clouds that were drifting down to overtake me. This precipice was drawing me to it, as if a rope were tied around my waist and pulling me up, up, up, but I was frightened to yield to the pull. I also immediately sensed that I was not alone; there were two beings with me, Jesus and Mary. We huddled together to discuss our course, and when I told them I was afraid to begin the journey, that I couldn't see but one step ahead of me because of the dense fog, Jesus said with complete

authority, "Follow me. I know the way *exactly*." He turned
and took off up the mountain. Startled and a bit panicked,
I looked to Mary as if to say, "Where's he going so fast?"
She smiled and said, "Keep your eyes on him, and I'll be
right behind you."

When I start after Jesus, it is as if my feet barely touch
the ground, as if it is no strain whatsoever to scale the
rocky trail. Soon we are moving so quickly, so surely, and
with such great agility that I am filled with exhilaration.
I have completely forgotten about the destination because
I am so entranced by the journey itself. The desire to keep
up with Jesus draws me forward. He is nearly flying up the
mountain, his eyes fixed ahead of him, seeing through the
fog what I am unable to see, and he moves over the rocks
without one misstep. I am aware of the strength in my legs
and of a quiet, unnameable strength that calls no attention to itself supporting me, carrying me up the hill. Mary,
trailing behind us, is so quiet, so silent, that I sometimes
think we have lost her. But when I turn around to check,
there she is, smiling and urging me to "just keep your eyes
on Jesus."

Mary's life, her vocation, her message, and her meaning have never been anything different from that—a gentle
beckoning to fix our eyes on the solution, the Shepherd, the
Savior who absolutely knows the way *exactly*. This is Mary
at the Annunciation: "Yes. Use me, without my knowing
the end result. Use me, set me to my heavenly task." This
is Mary whose spirit rejoices, "Great things he has done for

me!" This is Mary who pondered in her own heart, "And a sword shall pierce your own soul too." This is Mary at the wedding at Cana: "Do whatever he tells you." And this is Mary at the foot of the cross: an exposed and grippingly raw devotion, keeping her eyes on Jesus, even to the end.

Mary is not in competition with Jesus. She exists in support of him, and just as I was on my imaginary mountainside, she is in step right behind him. She was chosen and anointed and prepared for her vocation, and so am I. When heaven approached to announce her assignment, she accepted gladly; I can too. Her presence in my life has helped me grow as a woman, a Christian, and a Catholic. It took me some time and prayer and study and exploration to learn that she is not simply the fixed, pale, and powerless Madonna on the canvases of so many artists. She is my spiritual momma, the magnificent woman in the sky—powerful, willing, gentle, present, and capable. When I think of her, I think of her strength, her perseverance, her wisdom and purity. I am in awe of her power and of the position of grace, dignity, and influence that heaven bestowed upon her, which Christ confirmed and the church upholds.

This is Mary: woman, full of grace and blessed among all for generations, blessed because she *believed*. Surely this is our blessing too, if only we will say yes and keep our eyes on Jesus.

11

The Archangels: St. Michael, St. Gabriel, and St. Raphael

W E SING WITH THE ANGELS at every Mass. I don't know if other religions feature this option, but singing with angels is a pretty darn big draw to Catholicism for me.

This is how it works. During the Mass, just before beginning the Eucharistic prayer, the priest washes his hands as he prays, "Take away my iniquities, cleanse me of my sin." In this purified state, he then turns to the congregation and asks us to join the angels and saints in heaven, singing, "Holy, holy, holy Lord, God of power and might. Heaven and earth are full of your glory, hosanna in the highest. Blessed is he who comes in the name of the Lord, hosanna in the highest." It is a moment during which we consciously recognize that the world of the spirit and the corporeal world are intertwined.

Human beings are made up of body and spirit, but angels exist purely in spirit. The church teaches that "angels have intelligence and will: they are personal and immortal creatures, surpassing in perfection all visible creatures"

(*Catechism*, 330). They are servants and messengers of God. St. Basil wrote, "Beside each believer stands an angel as protector and shepherd leading him to life."

Angels play a leading role in my world as a Catholic. Not because they have recently become so fashionable but because they are embodiments of the creed's declaration that we believe in things "seen and unseen." Angels seem to fall somewhere in the middle—more often unseen, occasionally seen—and it is that deliciously murky area of our faith life that calls us into an awareness of other dimensions. Angels keep things interesting.

And they always seem to be in the thick of things. They tended to Jesus when he was fasting in the desert; they met Mary Magdalene at the empty tomb; they stayed the hand of Abraham when he was about to sacrifice his son, Isaac. They will accompany Christ when he returns and are given many specific appointments in the book of Revelation, such as sounding trumpets and raising incense. They surround God now in heaven and praise him eternally. It has great personal meaning for me, a singer, that angels apparently have been given the ability to sing, and that in addition to fighting evil and carrying messages, singing seems to be high on their eternal "to-do" list.

There are only three angels referred to in the Bible by name: Michael, the battling angel; Gabriel, whose role in the Annunciation brings him quickly to mind; and Raphael, who visited Tobit and Sarah and accompanied Tobias on his long journey. These three we refer to as archangels.

St. Michael

Never mind the circumstances. They are unimportant. Just know that I was walking out of Mass one day begging God to send me an angel because I was feeling very much under attack, vulnerable, and desperate for support. At the time, I did not frequently request the assistance of angels. I certainly believed in angels, but I rarely thought about them having direct contact with my world or intervening on my behalf in any direct way.

It was my habit upon returning to work from noon Mass to check my mailbox, which I did. Normally it would have been empty, but that day it had one little envelope. Inside, I found a prayer card for St. Michael the archangel, protector of God's people. Attached to the card was a short note from a coworker who, though we did not know each other very well, knew of my pressing situation. The note read, "This might seem cheesy, but I carry this prayer card in my shirt pocket. You can have it."

I call on heaven's angels, especially my guardian angel, with far more frequency now.

Hollywood could create no better superhero than St. Michael the archangel, the warrior angel. While he makes infrequent appearances in Scripture, he is featured in the book of Daniel, a wonderful read. He is assigned to protect God's people. There are numerous prayers to St. Michael; the most traditional begins, "Defend us in battle, be our defense against the wickedness and snares of the devil." These phrases bring me a greater sense of the resources

God makes available to me to fight the good fight, to lead a life of holiness.

St. Gabriel

Gabriel may be the best known of the three archangels, having visited Mary to announce her heavenly appointment in Luke's Gospel. St. Gabriel is the messenger angel, and in addition to announcing the incarnation of Christ and the pregnancy of Mary's cousin Elizabeth, who was believed to be barren, the angel Gabriel left Mary with these stirring and powerful words: "nothing will be impossible with God" (Luke 1:37). I can't help but believe that this message was more for us than for Mary. Mary probably already believed that, having been raised a faithful Jew. In any case, it is a wonderful phrase to ponder when seeking God's perfect will. I pray for the intercession of the angel Gabriel, especially when I'm seeking clear direction regarding my vocation or feeling called to a task beyond any ability I know myself to possess. *Show me how, Lord, for nothing is impossible with you.*

St. Raphael

As I've written, the church and elementary school of my childhood was named St. Raphael's, St. Ray's for short. So this archangel, the saint of happy meetings and good health, has always been a favorite. He is featured in the book of Tobit, another wonderful book from the Old Testament.

The angel Raphael was sent to heal the anguished Sarah, who was without a husband, and Tobit, who had lost his sight. Raphael carried the prayers of these distressed people directly "before the glory of the Lord" (Tobit 12:12). Disguised as a human, Raphael accompanied Tobit's son Tobias on an arduous journey that resulted in the marriage of Tobias and Sarah and the healing of Tobit.

The "love story" between the troubled Sarah and the skeptical Tobias is set into motion through the words of Raphael. He assures the nervous Tobias, "Do not be afraid, for she was set apart for you before the world was made." It is wonderful to read further in the passage that Tobias "loved her very much, and his heart was drawn to her" (Tobit 6:18). Those seeking spouses often call upon the prayers of St. Raphael.

One of the more beautiful prayers to St. Raphael is attributed to Ernest Hello and concludes with this wonderful line: "Remember the weak, you who are strong, you whose home lies beyond the region of thunder, in a land that is always peaceful, always serene and bright with the resplendent glory of God."

Angels are generally honored throughout the month of September. The collective feast day for the archangels Michael, Gabriel, and Raphael is September 29.

12

POPE JOHN PAUL II

H E WAS THE POPE OF my generation. Etched into the early years of my faith life will always be the early events of his papacy, dramatic and poignant, brought to my living room via the nightly news. An assassination attempt, a prolonged recovery, and later a quiet, heroic act of forgiveness. The picture is famous now, Pope John Paul II and his would-be assassin, sitting together in intimate conversation two years after the incident. The Holy Father, leaning toward the man with gentle attention, and later demonstrating extraordinary restraint in never revealing the contents of their conversation. It is a beautiful picture and the epitome of what makes Pope John Paul II unique in my view. He was unafraid of the vulnerability created by living in forgiveness, of sitting in total love with the enemy. It was a stunning paradox, and one he didn't just preach about from pulpits far removed from "real life," but one he lived right to the end.

It was March 12 of the Jubilee Year 2000 when Pope John Paul II made history by asking for forgiveness. Addressing an audience of thousands gathered at St. Peter's, the pope made a sweeping confession. Noting the Crusades, the Inquisition, and transgressions against Jews, women, and minorities, he said, "We humbly ask for forgiveness for the part that each of us with his or her behaviors has played in such evils thus contributing to disrupting the face of the church. At the same time, as we confess our sins let us forgive the faults committed by others towards us."

Some critics argued that this was simply a strategically planned exercise before the pope's visit to the war-torn Middle East, or the natural political inclination in the Jubilee Year, a traditional time to forgive all "debts." However, there was great and holy humility, as well as fearlessness, in his choice to publicly request forgiveness. Maybe it was the same holy humility that inspired Pope John Paul II to study for the priesthood underground during the Nazi occupation of Poland. Had his studies been discovered, it would have cost him his life, but his need for God was greater than his need for security. We can all learn from his example.

The centripetal forces of ecumenism and forgiveness behind his public act of repentance in March 2000, like the forgiveness he extended to his would-be assassin, are the same forces that fed his entire papacy. Christ chose Peter to serve as the rock upon which he would build his church, and Peter was martyred for it in the end. The pontiff is the natural successor of Peter, to whom Christ gave the power "to bind and to loose," and the post must be an impossibly difficult one. Pope John Paul II was loved deeply and hated bitterly. Millions prayed for his intentions daily, even as rock idols ripped up his picture on national television. In a world so fatherless, so abandoned by figures of strength and interior authority, we need a pope. We need to ask for the grace of repentance. We need to ask forgiveness and receive it. We need to offer it liberally and without charge to our neighbors, our enemies, our families, our governments, ourselves. Even while bearing the weight of the controversies that threaten to tear the church apart, from within and without, even while bearing the isolation that surely must come from carrying such a weight, Pope John Paul II uttered a constant refrain of fearless, abundant forgiveness born of love.

"Certainly forgiveness does not come spontaneously or naturally to people," he wrote. "Forgiving from the Heart can sometimes be heroic. . . . Thanks to the healing power of love, even the most wounded heart can experience the liberating encounter with forgiveness."

Yet asking for forgiveness in our culture is often seen as a supreme act of weakness, even foolhardy naïveté; the more popular attitude is "Never let 'em see you sweat." It robs us of our humanity to no longer recognize the truth that we are creatures who sin, creatures who need forgiveness and a Savior. This tragic false belief robs us of the very mechanism by which we might realize peace.

"Real peace is not just a matter of structures and mechanisms," wrote Pope John Paul II. "It rests above all on the adoption of a style of human coexistence marked by mutual acceptance and a capacity to forgive from the heart. We all need to be forgiven by others, so we must all be ready to forgive. Asking and granting forgiveness is something profoundly worthy of every one of us."

It is this message of reconciliation that John Paul took quite literally to the ends of the earth. (Global papal visits numbered 250 in the course of his papacy, not counting the audiences he gave within the Vatican to numerous heads of state, dignitaries, and others from around the world.) I believe it is this message that is helping re-anchor my generation: *Forgive us our trespasses as we forgive those who trespass against us.*

During the Jubilee Year, I had the opportunity to see the pope many times. One encounter will always stand out in my memory.

It was a rainy day in February, but the piazza at St. Peter's was still packed, weather never being any kind of deterrent to seeing the pope for so many pilgrims. We gathered together on cold black plastic chairs, trying to stay warm and secure a seat where we might get a close picture.

Just in front of the group with which I was sitting was an Italian family of five.

As the pontiff began to address the crowd, a woman in the family who seemed close to my age began weeping, and to my great surprise she pulled out a cell phone and quickly dialed a number. As the Holy Father's voice echoed out over the wet and shivering crowd, she said into the phone, "Mama, la voce del Papa" and held it up over her head.

We sat there in the rain and wept with her.

Indeed, his voice has been remarkable, if at times controversial, one that has carried the tender and beautiful messages of ecumenism, forgiveness, and redemption, one that has blessed my life and my faith in lasting, gentle, heroic ways. I will always miss him.

We pray for the repose of the soul of Pope John Paul II.

13

FLANNERY O'CONNOR

....

Dogma is the guardian of mystery.
—*Flannery O'Connor*

MANY ARTISTS AND WRITERS FIND their home in the liturgy and life of the Catholic Church, and through their various gifts they draw me back to experience what writer Luigi Guissani refers to as "the gaze of Christ." Flannery O'Connor is one of these artists. Her writing, both fiction and nonfiction, draws me to deeper relationship with Jesus in the mystery of the Eucharist and, in the more practical aspects, to deeper relationship with the church and faith. She is also a wonderful example of Catholic formation and a solid reminder that faith flourishes when it is reasoned and well educated.

O'Connor suffered from lupus and, like her father, died quite young. Yet she rarely complained of her illness or appeared to suffer from self-pity. Instead, she accepted her illness and the quiet self-imposed internment of her Georgia farm while occasionally poking fun at her deteriorating body. She wrote to a friend in 1956:

> I have never been anywhere but sick. In a sense
> sickness is a place, more instructive than a long
> trip to Europe, and it's always a place where there's
> no company, where nobody can follow. Sickness
> before death is a very appropriate thing and I
> think those who don't have it miss one of God's
> mercies.

The beauty of O'Connor's unaffected affliction is a powerful example of acceptance and the potential value of suffering. She was a woman self-possessed, even through the disappointment of illness and early death. Her faith was undoubtedly a cornerstone of such flat acceptance.

"The Church is mighty realistic about human nature," she wrote in a letter to a friend. So was O'Connor. Her fiction is often remembered for its depraved and selfish characters who commit violent acts with a dry pragmatism. It might be somewhat ironic, then, that her fiction helped me better appreciate the beauties of my faith. After finishing "A Good Man Is Hard to Find," the story of a family murdered on their way to vacation in Florida, I slammed my book shut and thought, *That is a story.* One of her most famous and most anthologized works, "A Good Man Is Hard to Find" cuts to the bone. Part of O'Connor's genius was in how she often found ways to bring the most cutting questions of faith and sin straight to the fore. She was unafraid of laying bare our most tender mysteries and human frailties, our ugliest weaknesses. "A Good Man Is

Hard to Find" is a brilliant example of this. One of its main characters, The Misfit, an escaped murderer who is about to kill again, says, "Jesus was the only One that ever raised the dead . . . and He shouldn't have done it. He thrown everything off balance." Part of the tragedy of The Misfit is not that he lacks knowledge of the works of Jesus, but more that he simply doesn't like the results. Like so many of O'Connor's characters, The Misfit does not mince words, and neither did O'Connor, particularly when she was expounding on her faith.

O'Connor was not only a finely formed writer (she completed her graduate studies at the highly regarded Iowa Workshop), but she was also a well-educated and finely formed Catholic. This is made most evident in the body of her nonfiction writing. She was a skilled essayist and prolific correspondent, especially when her illness confined her to her family farm in the latter years of her life. *Flannery O'Connor: Spiritual Writings,* edited by Robert Ellsberg, is a wonderful collection of her letters and writings. This medley of spiritual writings lays bare O'Connor's unpretentious, unaffected, and extremely well-formed faith.

Many an admiring reader frequently sought her counsel on matters of faith. In 1962, in a letter to a young student who was struggling with his beliefs, she wrote:

> One of the effects of modern liberal Protestantism
> has been gradually to turn religion into poetry
> and therapy, to make truth vaguer and vaguer

and more and more relative, to banish intellectual
distinctions, to depend on feeling instead of
thought, and gradually to come to believe that
God has no power, that he cannot communicate
with us, cannot reveal himself to us, indeed has
not done so, and that religion is our own sweet
invention. . . . Of course, I am a Catholic and I
believe the opposite of all this. I believe what the
Church teaches—that God has given us reason to
use and that it can lead us toward a knowledge of
him, through analogy; that he has revealed himself in history and continues to do so through the
Church, and that he is present (not just symboli-
cally) in the Eucharist on our altars. To believe all
this I don't take any leap into the absurd. I find
it reasonable to believe, even though these beliefs
are beyond reason. . . . Satisfy your demand
for reason always but remember that charity
is beyond reason, and that God can be known
through charity.

O'Connor is a Catholic for this season of church crises. As
churches are closing all around Boston, I read her words:
"It's in the nature of the church to survive all crises—in
however a battered fashion." She was free to observe the
church's struggles without it diminishing her faith in
God. In the same way, she could expose the flaws of her

characters without it diminishing her belief that no matter their choices, they were still divine creations of God. The immutable truth and enduring mystery of God's presence through the church never left her.

Without the least promise of glory or glamour, she invites others to reflect the world as it is, and to love it no less for its weaknesses.

> The novelist will have to do the best he can in travail with the world he has. He may find in the end that instead of reflecting the image at the heart of things, he has only reflected our broken condition and, through it, the face of the devil we are possessed by. This is a modest achievement, but perhaps a necessary one. ("Novelist and Believer")

O'Connor's faith was not easily ruffled, even when the underbelly of weakness and sin was exposed in her characters or the people around her. Instead, she clung to the understanding that the church was not to be measured by the imperfect souls who embraced it. She writes, "The Truth does not change according to our ability to stomach it emotionally." Nor was she afraid to live with the mystery of things: her own suffering; the reality of sin, grace, and salvation; and the real presence of Jesus in the Eucharist. She writes, "The Church's vision is prophetic vision; it is always widening the view. . . . The Church stands for and preserves always what is larger than human understanding."

I am grateful for her life, her work, and her faith, and the raw and practical yet mysterious ways that they widen our view.

14

The Young Thomas Merton
in Rome

W HEN I TRAVELED TO ROME on pilgrimage, I took only one book with me: Thomas Merton's auto- biography, *The Seven Storey Mountain*. A Trappist monk, remarkable scholar, and prolific author, Merton led a life of contemplation, prayer, writing, and social activism. While all of his work is deeply moving, his autobiography was my introduction to him and so remains my most beloved of his many writings. My favorite passage recalls his visit to Rome as a young man aloof to religion, much less Catholicism. As *The Seven Storey Mountain* was my introduction to Merton, Merton's trip to Rome was his introduction to Christ.

It was his second visit to the Eternal City. He was just about to enter university and was full of youthful hubris. He wrote of that time, "I imagined that I really was grown up and independent, and I could stretch out my hands and take all the things I wanted." Instead he found himself traveling with a stack of tattered novels, short of money, frequently cold, full of self-righteous indignation, and plagued by a painful boil on his elbow and an abscess under a tooth that a Roman dentist would later extract while Merton feared "death by anesthetic." Ah, glorious, glamorous independence!

But there was far more awaiting Merton in Rome than, ah, well, pus and a crushed hubris. Merton began visiting the many beautiful historic churches throughout Rome. He wrote that he was drawn to them by the Gospel story told through their art, "an art that was tremendously serious and alive and eloquent and urgent in all that it had to say." He spent his days wandering through these holy places as any pilgrim would, stopping to study, to learn, and to pay homage to the story their ancient masterpieces told over and over again with flat mosaic simplicity. "Thus without knowing anything about it," he acknowledged, "I became a pilgrim."

This is the Merton I remember and treasure most, the one faith sneaked up on. Not the internationally recognized contemplative scholar and activist he would later become, but the scruffy uncertain kid with a hole in his mouth where his abscessing tooth used to be, poor and full of questions, wandering the streets of the Eternal City. And there, for the first time, meeting Jesus.

So in my final days of pilgrimage in Rome—like Merton, running low on cash, and having grown accustomed to the pickpockets on Bus 64 and learned my way around sufficiently enough—I began to visit the churches that Merton visited. With my notebook, rosary, and *The Seven Storey Mountain* tucked into the recesses of my battered backpack, along with a few cans of low-sodium tuna, I went from church to church, underlining each one in my book as I went. It was my own little "pilgrimage within a pilgrimage." My Merton pilgrimage.

It seemed fitting enough: an aspiring writer and Catholic literally following in the footsteps of another who wanted to be so much more than he was at the time, a young man discovering Jesus. For in Rome, he said, "my conception of Christ was formed. It was there I first saw Him, Whom I now serve as my God and my King, and Who owns and rules my life." And both of us followed in the footsteps of so many generations of martyrs and believers: St. Peter, St. Paul, and all the rest who gave their lives over to Christ and to martyrdom. I felt stirred with deep conviction and purpose as I walked the forgotten cobbled streets that led to Santa Prassede and Santa Pudenziana, climbing the stairs that led to San Pietro in Vincoli.

I ferreted out those same "lesser" churches, the smaller churches, less grandiose and obvious than the awesome palaces like St. Peter's. I studied the same mosaics, some restored, some deteriorating, some buried beneath scaffolding, in the process of being cleaned and restored. I knelt at the same railings and prayed my prayers and wrote for hours and hours in my notebook while my fingers froze and my nose turned red. And I asked Merton, wherever he was, writer to writer, "Pray for me."

Finally, one sunny March day, I climbed the Aventine hill to visit Merton's Santa Sabina. Breathless and warm from climbing the hill in my wool coat, I entered the church where Merton said he prayed for one of the first times in his life. Merton recalled that he kneeled self-consciously at the altar in the company of one little old Italian lady and prayed one Our Father, "slowly, with all the belief I had in me."

It was the last of my "Merton churches," and I sat for several hours there contemplating my return to the United States and all that had transpired during my time in Rome. I thought about Merton and all that had transpired for him and how much had yet to unfold for him in his journey of faith, bright and breathtaking and heartbreaking and humbling all at the same time.

What I didn't know was that in a few hours penitential services would be held at Santa Sabina, and I would be struck with a deep grief. A cry would rise up from me and would not cease repeating: "Lord, don't forget me, just don't forget me." I would write in my journal that I was "in scorching pain."

The penitential chant did not break for an hour or more, and only during adoration, when a guitarist at the front of the church, who had played only hymns throughout the evening, started to play, with utter reverence, "All the Things You Are." It was a Jerome Kern tune I had sung hundreds of times in jazz clubs. That I was hearing it here was bizarre and unlikely and wonderful. I started to sing along, "You are the angel glow that lights a star, the dearest things I know are what you are. And some day, my happy arms will hold you, and some day I'll know the moment divine when all the things you are are mine." And I wondered if God, as he had on so many occasions, was speaking to me through music. As Merton did in the mosaics, Jesus came to visit me in music, in that lovely Santa Sabina on the top of the Aventine hill—where Merton and I had both prayed with as much belief as we could muster.

Merton once wrote that he—briefly—had ambitions to become a jazz musician and was relieved when later in life he realized that pursuing that particular vocation might have been detrimental to his soul. Eventually Merton became a Trappist monk and authored numerous books. He entered into hidden, silent, mystic life, a life I certainly cannot tell in a few pages. But I give thanks for it. His candid autobiography helped launch me into a new phase of my own faith experience—what he might have called "a capitulation, a surrender"—because he so humbly allows us to enter into his, without pretense, without fakery, without spiritual bells and whistles parading as piety.

He would likely tell you himself that he was no saint—and it comes as some relief to me that he wasn't. I love Merton not so much for where he ended up on the world's scale of things, but for where he started. When it comes to my own pilgrimage, I want to take the quiet roads that lead to greater contemplation—not of the architectural feats of emperors and kings, but of the sanctifying feats of

God, the restoration of souls lost, haggard, worn down, in need of great repair, like all those ancient mosaics, still so alive and "urgent in all that they have to say."

One day I plan to go back to Rome to spend more time with Merton and the churches where he said he first met Christ. Maybe by then I will be a better writer, a better Catholic, a better contemplative, and I will have, in some small way, Merton and the "lesser" churches of Rome to thank for it.

And that jazz guitarist in Santa Sabina.

15

MARY LOU WILLIAMS
AND THE BLESSING OF CONVERSION

SHE WAS A JAZZ PIANIST, a composer, an arranger, an educator, and a devout humanitarian. A convert to Catholicism in the later years of her life, Mary Lou Williams had a tremendous influence on jazz when few women had such opportunity. Her musical life started with tumult and ended peacefully within the realm of the spirit. Her conversion is a moving testimony to the saving, transforming power of God.

From birth, Williams appeared to be marked for an unusual life, perhaps a life better fitted to a mystic than a musician. Growing up in egregious neglect, alcoholism, abuse, poverty, and loneliness, Williams often had terrifying visions in which she saw ghosts and spirits. But God in his mercy provides his most tender creatures with means to cope with such evil. For Williams, it was music.

She taught herself the piano before she was five years old. Noted jazz biographer Linda Dahl writes in the beautiful book *Morning Glory: A Biography of Mary Lou*

Williams that some of Williams's earliest attachments to music were of a spiritual nature. She would often stand underneath the window of a local Catholic school for girls and listen while the choir practiced. "To Mary," writes Dahl, "their singing was 'angelic' and had a deep influence that revealed itself years later when she began to write choral jazz and sacred works."

Within a few years, Williams, still a child, earned the name "the Piano Girl of East Liberty." She began playing for tea parties, galas, and churches throughout Pittsburgh and eventually left home as a teenager to begin her life on the road as a jazz musician. She was quickly recognized as a "musician's musician" and a composer, arranging in the male-dominated world of big band for the likes of Duke Ellington and Benny Goodman. She would keep company with, and often serve as instructor to, other jazz legends, such as Thelonious Monk, Dizzy Gillespie, Charlie Parker, Erroll Garner, and Bud Powell, to mention but a few. It was not uncommon for players, after gigs at Birdland in New York, to assemble in Williams's apartment to play into the early morning hours. Often Williams offered instruction to other players coming up through the bebop era, when pianists often used their left hand for light comping and their right for flying solos. Johnnie Garry, a manager at Birdland, remembers Williams sitting at the piano with Bud Powell, rapping his hand with a ruler and saying, "Left hand, Bud, left hand." She "played heavy like a man," and it was perhaps this weighty presence that helped her survive the grueling lifestyle.

Like so many talented jazz musicians of that era, Williams was often destitute and rarely collected royalties for her work. She had the added tribulation of suffering at the hands of crooked managers and drunken lovers and husbands. Eventually, following years of living on the road and generally demoralized by ill treatment, Williams found herself at rock bottom. Stranded in Europe with no money and no means to return to the United States, she was befriended by a wealthy American patron.

This devout Catholic introduced Mary to a quiet church in Paris with a walled garden. Williams returned to the garden later on her own and while there experienced a stirring vision of the Virgin Mary. She noted that it was the most powerful supernatural vision of her life. Shortly thereafter, along with Lorraine Gillespie, the wife of Dizzy Gillespie, Williams took instruction in Catholicism and entered the church in 1957. She was never disturbed with ghostly visions again, and her years spent in the church were some of the most peaceful of her entire life.

Jazz saved her from despair in her early life, and her conversion served to illuminate her jazz compositions in later life. After becoming Catholic, Williams wrote and arranged a jazz Mass and numerous liturgical works, including one that was commissioned by the Vatican. Williams said, "Jazz is healing to the soul. . . . I'm praying through my fingers when I play. I think the entire world is kind of upset, and I don't think people know very much what to do with themselves. . . . I make it by sticking with my work and thinking that everything's going to be OK—which I think it will be."

More important than providing new subject matter for her compositions, her faith also served to strengthen her playing. Williams's biographer, Linda Dahl, comments, "Always there was her faith to help her. And her music. Personal upheavals had not the slightest effect on the power of Mary's music making. . . . Not that she disguised her conflicts and pain but her dark side was transformed, lending tremendous vitality to her playing. She constructed her solos, said one reviewer, 'like small dramas of the spirit in search of light.'"

Ellington once said that Williams's music was like "soul on soul." In the end, she was comforted by her faith in Jesus and the music that helped bring him to her. She once wrote this note on a scrap of paper: "Jazz created for all people. Jazz created through suffering." In a way, her tender thoughts encapsulate the Gospel message she came to believe: Jesus suffered, once for all, for us and for our salvation. Her life, her faith, and her music captured the essence of the transformation we all hope for as God's children, little spirits in search of light.

16

THE COMMUNION OF SAINTS

....

S T. MARGARET OF CORTONA HAD a child out of wed-
lock and was mistress to a man she eventually found
murdered, hidden and decaying in the woods. St. Paul persecuted Christians as Saul before his conversion. St. Joseph
of Cupertino couldn't get a job, St. Thomas doubted, and
St. Peter denied Christ three times, his apparent failing
and fear recorded for all posterity, not once but four times,
in the New Testament.

Most saints did not have easy lives. Many were persecuted and martyred. They were an odd lot, many of them
outcasts who experienced every kind of human suffering
and weakness. And many of them began as ordinary folks
like you and me.

The saints became most real to me when I was in Rome.
In the Eternal City it was impossible to avoid the homage paid to relics of every kind from every kind of saint.
No city more readily celebrates the lives and deaths of the
saints. Relics, which were originally cherished as a means

of strengthening faith among the persecuted, are available for viewing in churches on nearly every street corner. Contemporary Catholics still venerate relics of the saints. Of course, St. Peter's Basilica is built over what is believed to be the actual bones of the saint himself. I have had the privilege of being closer to them than most people.

Toward the end of my stay in Rome, I had the extraordinary opportunity to walk through the excavation two stories below St. Peter's. In order to preserve the fragile remains, the excavation would soon be closing to the general public. Understanding this only heightened the anticipation I shared with the handful of others who accompanied me. We had spent so many weeks working in the magnificent structure that is St. Peter's Basilica; it seemed somewhat surreal that we'd soon be standing at the actual tomb that had inspired it.

A priest from the North American Seminary led us down into the darkness. An accomplished historian, he knew every detail of the excavation and informed us that the necropolis below St. Peter's was discovered in 1939 just as World War II was beginning to take over Europe. Throughout the war, the excavation was carried out in secret in order to avoid desecration of the tombs. It was completed in 1950 when Pope Pius XII announced to the world that the tomb of St. Peter, a point of veneration for Christians from the first century forward, had been found.

We wove our way through the catacombs. We examined ancient mosaics and discussed ancient burial practices.

We breathed the cold still air and collectively fell silent when we finally came to the tomb of St. Peter.

After a few minutes, Father led us in prayer. We remembered silently all the petitions that had brought us on this pilgrimage in the first place. We stood on that holy ground, just inches from St. Peter's tomb, and remembered our loved ones and the petitions rising up from the deepest parts of our hearts. We cried and stood hovering together in the rocky cavern, complete strangers just moments ago, now suddenly united, a family, a communion of believers with the same hopes and fears and prayers and capacity to love. It was not where we started, but it was where we ended up, crouching together underneath a veritable mountain of marble and stone.

It is not where many of the saints started but where they ended up that gives me courage. Prior to the Edict of Milan in AD 313, when Christianity was no longer outlawed, the saints were by and large those who had been martyred, often publicly and violently, for their faith. Saints were still made after the edict, but sainthood began to take on a different flavor. Where martyrdom had once been one of the chief markers of saints, now holiness became a sign of saintliness, and this holiness was measured by good works and a life of love, service, and heroic virtue.

In *Making Saints: How the Catholic Church Determines Who Becomes a Saint, Who Doesn't, and Why,* Kenneth Woodward writes:

A saint is always someone through whom we catch
a glimpse of what God is like—and of what we are
called to be. Only God "makes" saints, of course.
The church merely identifies from time to time a
few of these for emulation. The church then tells
the story. But the author is the Source of the grace
by which saints live. And there we have it: A saint
is someone whose story God tells.

The story God tells over and over in his saints is this: sainthood is not reserved for perfect people; instead, we are all,
in varying stages, a part of the communion of saints.

Hovering over us in this great communion are people
such as St. Gianna Beretta Molla, a doctor and mother who
gave her own life to save the life of her baby; St. Katharine
Drexel, who gave up millions of dollars and a life of luxury
and privilege in order to serve Indians and blacks in the
United States; St. Padre Pio, who bore the stigmata; and
St. Joseph, head of the holy family, whose quiet and just
presence protected Mary and Jesus even as kings tried to
murder them. I have my own favorites whom I call on to
intercede for my causes. (Some of them are included in
this book.) In the same way that I might ask my mother—
whose faith, devotion, and fervency I admire—to pray for
me, I might also ask St. Ann, the mother of Mary, to pray
for my intentions. From the stories of the saints, I garner
strength and inspiration, and I remember that saints are
ordinary people who managed to do heroically loving

things by cooperating with the grace of God. In doing so, the saints bridge earth and heaven, and heaven rushes down, anxious to greet us, anxious to wash over us and draw us into communion.

I am quite certain that the church will not be telling my "story" someday. But I am oh-so-grateful to be given the chance to play a part, even a small part, in that graceful heavenly communion.

We celebrate All Saints' Day on November 1.

St. Peter, pray for us.

17

THE SWISS GUARD

I T'S LIKE SOMETHING OUT OF a Hollywood epic. In a most complicated and dark time—complete with warring factions, mercenaries out of control, and politicians and rulers and religious leaders at odds (some struggling for power and wealth, others for more virtuous ends)—strength of character, strength of conviction, and strength of hand combined to defend the Sacrament. On May 6, 1527, armies under the rule of Emperor Charles V attacked and pillaged the Vatican and Rome in one of the more brutal and notorious sacks of Rome. In the end, 147 of the 189 Swiss Guards who had taken an oath to protect Pope Clement VII lost their lives. In eight days, an estimated twelve thousand Romans—men, women, and children—were slaughtered. Tombs and relics and sacred works of art were plundered and desecrated, but Pope Clement was saved.

The Swiss Guards had been invited to Rome as "defenders of the church's freedom" only a few years earlier by Pope Julius II, in 1506. These men were recognized as cunning and worthy warriors who had developed the most sophisticated fighting tactics of their time, which allowed them to do battle with and resist armies of far greater numbers. Perhaps more important, they were "renowned for their courage, noble sentiments, and loyalty."

May 6 is the day when new guards are sworn in at the Vatican. In this moving ceremony, young Roman Catholic men promise fidelity to the pope and the church while raising three fingers of their right hand—those symbolizing the Father, the Son, and the Holy Spirit.

Because of the courage and valor they demonstrated centuries ago, this unique Swiss regiment has guarded every pope since the early 1500s. They are responsible for the pontiff's physical safety when he travels outside the Vatican and for the security at the Apostolic Palace, the papal apartment, and the four main entrances to the Vatican.

My first encounter with a Swiss Guard was during the Jubilee Year when I volunteered in Rome. We worked half days and were left with plenty of time to explore the city. One of my favorite spots to pray in my off hours was St. Ann's Chapel, just inside the Vatican walls. I discovered quickly that because St. Ann's is a part of Vatican City, you can only visit it during certain hours. If you were found wandering into Vatican City at unauthorized times, those magnificently cloaked young men would turn you right around. Don't let their colorful tights or refined manner fool you. You don't want to mess with a member of the Swiss Guard.

That sentiment is really appealing to me. For starters, the story of the Swiss Guard's heroism reminds me of some of the things that I most admire about men. Call me old-fashioned, but I am drawn to a man who's got a bit of warrior in him, who's willing to put it all on the line. That kind of courage is shunned in our culture sometimes, even "diagnosed" as aggression or hyperactivity or worse. When misplaced or mismanaged, any gift we've been given by God can be distorted and become destructive. Strength can brutalize, or it can save. Confidence can uplift, or it can swell into arrogance that crushes others. I believe the history of the Swiss Guard speaks to an essential, intrinsic element of man's constitution. Men were born to fight for something they believe in, to use their strength to protect and defend and build, to take pride in their calling, in who they were created to be, and in the courage of their hearts. I wish our culture celebrated men more for the potentially, wonderfully dangerous creatures they are.

Christ, after all, was no shrinking violet. When soldiers came to hunt him down in the Garden of Gethsemane, he stood his ground. By merely saying, "I am he," he knocked those soldiers armed with clubs and swords back and to the ground. His sheer presence was that overwhelming. He never denied who he was, and he didn't flinch, although the temptation to run and hide must have been lurking within.

While greatly outnumbered during the sack of Rome in 1527, the Swiss Guard stayed their ground and sacrificed their lives. Their oath—to be who they were—was more valuable to them than their physical lives. Their strength found its rightful place. In his book *Wild at Heart,* John Eldredge writes of men in our present-day culture: "Many of us have actually been afraid to let our strength show up because the world doesn't have a place for it. Fine. The world's screwed up. Let people feel the weight of who you are and let them deal with it."

That's an intriguing, even delicious thought. I am reminded of it when I look at my pictures of the Swiss Guards and think of when they wouldn't let me pass. They let the world feel their weight because they know who they are. This is not an act of arrogance or aggression or violence; it is the act of inhabiting oneself as created by God, our heavenly Father, with divine and eternal purpose and weight. And it certainly does not restrict itself only to males.

Though few of us will ever be called to sacrifice our lives to defend the faith, we are all called at times to let people feel our weight as Catholics. And sometimes that's uncomfortable; it requires a great deal of strength, strength cultivated and informed by the Holy Spirit. Then, in knowing ourselves and our passions so well, using them in God's service becomes far more important and interesting (even, dare I say, *adventurous*) than "making nice."

It would be absurd and unseemly to romanticize or glamorize war or the horrific and cowardly debaucheries like terrorism that have haunted our times and tried to ruin our families and economies and futures. Strength uninformed by courage, conviction, and rightness of heart is full of potential to become senseless violence. On the other hand, strength that is cultivated by the Holy Spirit, like any other important virtue, has the potential to change and save lives. The *Catechism* teaches that "the spiritual tradition of the Church also emphasizes the *heart,* in the biblical sense of the depths of one's being, where the person decides for or against God" (368). We are in desperate need of warriors who are *deciding for God.* How magnificent that we have been given this living example, a regiment chosen, set apart, armed, and ready—and deciding for God.

For "dangerous" men everywhere.

18

ST. JOSEPH OF CUPERTINO

....

WERE IT POSSIBLE FOR ME to choose just one saint as a favorite, it would be St. Joseph of Cupertino. I discovered him quite by accident when I accepted a writing assignment from a Franciscan magazine to write a short biography of a Franciscan saint. They gave me a brief list of saints who had not been covered in previous issues, and St. Joseph was on the roster. I skipped right past his name—I'm embarrassed to say that I'd never heard of him. Happily, that night, our paths crossed.

That summer, I made a meager living writing and working on a horse farm, where I exercised and cared for a string of polo ponies. Having grown up with horses, I loved working with these ponies. They were a source of comfort, and caring for them brought me peace. They were in the forefront of my mind the evening I went looking for information on lesser-known Franciscan saints. As chance would have it, I happened upon a short biography of St. Joseph of

Cupertino. Reading his story, I felt an immediate connection and delight. He was a horseman too, of sorts.

Born in the Italian village of Cupertino, St. Joseph was both an outcast and an oddity from the very beginning. His father died before Joseph was born, and his mother blamed young Joseph for the loss of her husband and rejected him because of it. Because she could not pay her taxes, she had to forfeit her house, and Joseph was born in a shed behind the house. Growing up in poverty, neglect, and abuse, young Joseph developed an unusual absentmindedness. He wandered through his village open-mouthed as if in a trance and was often referred to as "the Gaper" by other villagers.

Young Joseph didn't seem to fit in anywhere. He struggled as a young man to secure a vocation; his forgetfulness and clumsiness made him a poor worker. It seemed the harder he tried, the more disgruntled people became with him. He had failed at several apprenticeships—including shoemaking and dishwashing—and was completely rejected by his mother and community. Out of what must have been utter frustration, Joseph developed a raging temper. He continued to struggle in various appointments and vocations, never finding his place. He was truly a lost and lonely soul.

But then, through the influence of an uncle who was a Conventual priest (though some histories record that it was an aunt who was a nun), Joseph was offered a tertiary habit in the Franciscan Order and was assigned to work in the stables. There, in the company of those gentle beasts and in the humility of simple daily labors, St. Joseph underwent a moving conversion and a profound deepening of his faith. He became noted for his sweet temperament, innocence, and extraordinary fervor. He would fall into ecstasies at the slightest mention of the Lord. On more than seventy occasions, he levitated, often while saying Mass.

Sadly, even life as a mystic was full of struggle for St. Joseph. More than two hundred saints in the history of the church have levitated, but none so often as St. Joseph. As people began to hear of the "flying friar," his mystical experiences became a burden, attracting crowds of the curious and the critical.

As a result, he continued to be rejected by many as an oddity, even within the church. He was questioned by popes and other superiors and underwent a great period of aridity in his prayer life, which led to serious depression. He was isolated and lonely, and the friars eventually built him a private chapel off of his room so he could say Mass. There was a steep price to be paid for his moments of ecstasy, and more often than not, it was isolation.

When I am tempted by self-pity, I remember the "flying friar" and what must have been a truly lonely life at times. He is an inspiration to anyone who is suffering rejection, struggling to find his or her true vocation, or attempting to lift his or her thoughts more often toward heaven. And who among us has not experienced one or all of those things? In this way, I think St. Joseph of Cupertino is truly a saint for everyone.

Not too surprisingly, he is the patron saint of air travelers and pilots. He is also patron saint to students and astronauts.

Pray for us, St. Joseph, that through your gentle, innocent example, we may cultivate a greater levity of spirit, a finer clarity in our vocation, and a more fervent devotion to the Father, Son, and Holy Spirit.

19

Bd. Pier Giorgio Frassati

He was handsome, popular, athletic, educated, and wealthy; he also lived privately within the well-worn groove that leads to sainthood.

Though he died at the age of twenty-four, a victim of polio likely contracted while visiting the poor, Bd. Pier Giorgio Frassati had touched the lives of so many that thousands of mourners, the sick and the poor, flooded the streets of Turin for his funeral procession. His own family was surprised to discover that the hidden life of this burgeoning young mystic was a tireless gift of service and self-sacrifice.

Pier Giorgio's beatification inspires the devotion of many, especially university students and athletes. Part of what makes him so attractive is how exuberantly he embraced and lived life. He climbed mountains, rode horses, and was an avid cyclist; he enjoyed spending time with friends at the theater; he loved art, opera, and literature and could quote long passages of Dante. The son of a prominent businessman and politician who was also an agnostic, Pier Giorgio seemed well groomed for earthly living. Much to the surprise of the Turinese elite surrounding him, including his own family, Pier Giorgio was, as it turns out, "in the world and not of it." Like many of the saints of the church, Pier Giorgio seemed to lead two lives, not contradictory lives, but one that people observed and one that was hidden.

In public, he was involved in many social and political organizations that promoted the teachings of the Catholic Church, such as the Catholic Student Federation and the Catholic Worker Movement. He often expressed the sentiment that "charity is not enough; we need social reform." He publicly demonstrated against the Fascism of his day.

Pier Giorgio was the first to take action when necessary, no matter the cost to himself. For example, when Pier Giorgio graduated, his father gave him a choice of money or a car as a graduation present. He took the money and then quickly distributed it to the poor. Another time, on a cold night when the temperature dropped well below zero, Pier Giorgio gave the coat off his back to a man who had none, much to the chagrin of the elder Frassati. While Pier Giorgio could have afforded to take first-class trains, he often rode in the third-class car. When his friends asked him why he chose third class, he would reply, "Because there isn't a fourth." On the surface, Pier Giorgio was dedicated to social reform and to a life of generosity and humility.

It wasn't until the time of his death and afterward that much more was revealed about Pier Giorgio's hidden life of service and deep prayer. Secretly, he had kept a ledger of the numerous poor and sick he had helped and their various needs. On his deathbed, he passed along instructions to his sister so that she could continue his good works with those who had come to depend upon him. Pier Giorgio also experienced an unusual piety in his prayer life. He would sometimes spend the entire night on his knees in deep adoration before the Blessed Sacrament. He was devoted to the Blessed Mother and the rosary, saying the joyful, sorrowful, and glorious mysteries daily.

Quietly, this young, handsome man, born into wealth and privilege and education and advantage, had become saint material in small, daily, surreptitious ways. What does this mean to you and to me?

While the story of Pier Giorgio's life is a blessing and a challenge, it's more than a story, more than an example to be admired from a distance and then tucked neatly back on the shelf. His life, like Christ's, is an invitation, and that is what sainthood is. (For more on this, see chapter 16, "The Communion of Saints.") It is no small miracle when an ordinary person invites us to see the extraordinary in the world around us and beyond. Saints are people who invite us all to come and sit in the wonder of our Creator and to share in the grace of faith fed by love, humility, sacrifice, and piety. From that point of view, we can accomplish great things, real things, more than we ever could on our own. From the point of view of love and wonder, we can see where and how to enter the well-worn groove that leads to sainthood.

Pier Giorgio is a vivid reminder that sainthood is not reserved for monks living cloistered lives of private prayer, or for martyrs who gave up their bodies to the cruelest forms of brutality. Sainthood is a state of grace for all who avail themselves of God's holy fire of heart, allowing it to burn, burn, burn, right through to the core. Because of his willingness to walk such a sanctified path, to take the love of Jesus to the streets of Turin, Pier Giorgio was beatified by Pope John Paul II in May 1990.

Recently exhumed as part of the canonization process, Pier Giorgio's body was found incorrupt. This means that his body had not become subject to ordinary physical decay—a sure sign of his extraordinary holiness.

His feast day is July 4.

Bd. Pier Giorgio, pray for us.

The Imitation of Christ,
by Thomas à Kempis

A PRIEST TOLD ME ONCE that when Pope John Paul II went on retreat, he took only two books with him: the Bible and *The Imitation of Christ*. It may or may not be true, but I like the sentiment behind the notion. *The Imitation of Christ*, a collection of prayers, meditations, and reflections written by the fifteenth-century monk Thomas à Kempis, is one of the most popular and beloved spiritual works of all time. And hey, if it's good enough for the pope, it's good enough for me.

The Imitation of Christ contains one of my favorite quotes, though I didn't even know it did until recently. I first read the quote this way: "Circumstances do not make the man; they reveal him." I was delighted and surprised one day as I was flipping through *Imitation*'s pages to see the quote this way: "The time of adversity shows who is of most virtue. Occasions do not make a man frail, but they do show openly what he is." The quote sits on my desk now, begging higher virtue from me than I even wish to possess most days.

At the recommendation of a priest, I first began reading *Imitation* on my commute into Harvard every day, a twenty- to thirty-minute trip on a quiet trackless trolley. The prose of *Imitation* is so fierce at times that twenty to thirty minutes' worth is about as much as I can ingest in a sitting. It's a tough work. Not for the lighthearted. The first time I picked it up years and years ago, it felt so condemning and harsh that I didn't make it past the first few pages.

But as Harold Gardiner, S.J., wrote in 1955 in his introduction to the work, it is important to keep in mind when reading *The Imitation of Christ* that it does not contain the totality of the faith, but only a portion of it. It is a work "written by a monk for monks," and for monks living in a rather dark period of the church's history, when great self-mortification was commonly practiced. With maturing faith and a deeper understanding of the work, I now find it reassuring, illuminating, even joyful at times. We all have our "seasons" for things, and it is a Thomas à Kempis season for me.

Readers might also bear in mind that some of the words, when taken out of context of the day in which they were written, might have entirely different meanings today. Gardiner offers the word *vile* as an example. He suggests that the contemporary meaning of *vile*—"disgusting" or "repellent"—would be out of place in Thomas à Kempis's day. Instead, à Kempis used the word *vile,* in reference to the body as corruptible, to mean "of little worth." You may find it beneficial to read several translations along with the scholarly introductions that often accompany them in order to garner a more complete picture of the work and the context and culture of its creation. Gardiner writes, "It is to be taken, not as a complete explanation of the Catholic faith, but as a series of meditations to deepen one's interior life." It has now become my habit to pray one of his most fervent prayers each morning, the entirety of which can be summed up in these two sentences: "Put me where You will, and freely do with me in all things according to Your will. I am Your creature, and in Your hands; lead me and turn me where You will."

There has been some debate as to the authorship of *Imitation* over the centuries, but it is widely accepted at present that the work does belong to Thomas à Kempis. He was born near Düsseldorf in 1379 or 1380, during a period of especial tumult in the Christian community. The church was experiencing inordinate religious laxity and bewilderment as it struggled with authority and faithfulness. Popes and antipopes were no help in dealing with the various heresies of the day.

At age twelve, Thomas à Kempis left home and joined a religious community called the Brothers of the Common Life. There he learned Latin and copied manuscripts along with the community, whose primary aims were to strengthen general education among people, deepen religious life, and, as much as was possible, imitate the lives of the early Christians. At age nineteen, he discerned a vocation for religious life, and at thirty-three he was ordained a priest and entered into a more specifically monastic way of life.

Imitation has received criticism for being "nonintellectual," but it may be the very simple prose and approach to faith that has made it universally accessible and popular across continents and cultures. "Man is born up from earthly things on two wings, simplicity and purity," he wrote. "Simplicity is in the intention; purity is in the *love*." For all his own sound education, à Kempis was clearly interested in leading his fellow monks down the road of simple self-knowledge as a means for growing closer to God.

The practical, compassionate approach to intellectual pursuits in *Imitation* is also welcome in any language. At a time when education came at a premium for a select few, it was probably comforting for the masses to read, "Well-ordered learning is not to be belittled, for it is good and comes from God, but a clean conscience and a virtuous life are much better and more to be desired." And available to anyone, no matter his or her station.

The Imitation of Christ is at times reminiscent of the psalms in tone and timbre; Thomas cries out from a heart desperately in love with, in need of, the Almighty, and like the psalmist he recognizes the power in the one to whom he cries. Resembling the rhythm of the monastic chant that he must have practiced, à Kempis raises an impassioned plea:

> My Lord Jesus . . . come quickly and help me, for
> vain thoughts have risen in my heart and worldly
> fears have troubled me sorely. How shall I break
> them down? How shall I go unhurt without Your
> help? . . .
>
> Command the winds and the tempests of pride
> to cease; bid the sea of worldly covetousness to
> be at rest; and charge the northern wind—that
> is the devil's temptation not to blow. Then great
> tranquillity and peace will be within me. Send out
> Your light and Your truth of spiritual knowledge,
> that it may shine upon the earth, barren and dry.
> Send down Your grace from above, and with it
> anoint my dry heart.

I am grateful for this work and many other Catholic classics like it, which offer precious glimpses into the intimate relationship that my brothers and sisters in the faith have formed with Jesus, and these works, in their season, "anoint my dry heart" too.

Thomas à Kempis died July 25, 1471, at the age of ninety-two.

PART THREE

Devotion in Practice

21

May Crowning

....

It is my first "Catholic" memory and my first memory as a Catholic: May Crowning. The songs are still—and always—in my head.

> Hail, holy Queen enthroned above, oh Maria.
> Hail, mother of mercy and of love, oh Maria.
> Triumph all ye cherubim, Sing with us ye
>   seraphim.
> Heaven and earth resound the hymn.
> Salve, Salve, Salve Regina.

I wish that all children were welcomed into the fold of Catholic faith with the innocence and tenderness of singing seraphim, with a mother of mercy and love.

One of the defining aspects of being Catholic is devotion to Mary. I favor no Marian celebration more highly than May Crowning, the feast that recognizes Mary as queen of heaven and earth. To a person of any age, this is a mighty big title, but to a child of five or six or seven, it expands to enchanting, magical proportions. How many queens does one get a chance to meet in a lifetime, much less crown?

Thus, preparing for the May Crowning procession each spring at St. Raphael's, the church of my childhood, was a monumental and joyful task. My imagination may be filling in some of the details, but this is what I remember most. We practiced "Immaculate Mary" and "Hail, Holy Queen" until we knew the lyrics by heart. We girls put on our spring dresses and white tights, the boys their scratchy Sunday shirts and ties. We practiced "processing" with dignity and grace and with as few wiggles and squirms as our young bodies could manage. Some lucky second-grade girl would be chosen to crown Mary, not based on merit, but rather based entirely on whether she fit into the dress one of the local women had made for the ceremony many years earlier.

The rest of the children at St. Raphael's were assigned a very simple but very important role in the procession: we were each charged with bringing one flower to place at Mary's feet. We would literally cover the area around her in flowers, pretty much the most charming and romantic expression my young heart could imagine. I took on the selection of my flower with zeal: it was serious business, not to be dashed off quickly. The consideration required time and precision; like young parents trying to name their firstborn child, I thought about the future of the flower. How would it look lying prostrate as it was bunched with all the other local flora of the season? Would it hold its shape, its scent, its crowning beauty? Would it be worthy?

Spring came late to rural Minnesota. In the month of May, tulips were the first flowers to spring from the patch of garden in front of our garage. My mother (her name also Mary) planted them. As a five-year-old, I hovered over that patch of flora, examining each early bud while my large and loud family waited impatiently in the car. Finally, my mother, who often bore the brunt of my family's size and volume and impatient energy, said, "Just hurry up and pick one."

It was a strain to make a choice under such duress, but I finally settled on one pink and one yellow tulip—one flower for the Virgin Mary, and one flower for my mother, Mary. Scrubbed and dressed, with tights pulled up, and armed with my two prized tulips, I joined my brother and sisters in the backseat of our brown-paneled station wagon, and Dad drove us off to St. Raphael's.

Once there, and with as much pageantry and pomp as a farming community church could muster, we processed away, singing our "Ave Maria" and crowning our Mary while the angels kept us company. I imagined angels turned out in especially big numbers for Marian events, those "singing seraphim" that seemed often to appear in Mary's songs. I still think of that church as filled with angels, country angels, angels meant to protect country people, whose days were spent in labor over soil and crops and barnyard animals. Simple angels for simple people, scrubbed squeaky-clean for Mary and the Mass. I still remember the aroma of flowers, the coolness of the spring air, the lightness of spirit that lingered. The promise of everything made new.

May Crowning marked a new spiritual season. Our Mary, queen of heaven and earth, lifted us right out of the last long, cold days of winter and firmly planted our hearts in the warm and promising soil of spring.

I will be forever grateful to the church for bringing me Mary, and grateful to Mary for bringing me her Son. For that was my route. I might not have discovered the gaze of Jesus if I had not first felt the maternal, nurturing, and safe embrace of my mother in heaven. That's why we crown her on our Catholic version of Mother's Day. That's why I hovered over the tulips in front of the garage looking for just the right one. Through Mary, I became enamored of the holy family. Through Mary, I was invited into the Catholic fold. It was her feminine presence and the safety of her motherhood that helped me grow. My child's heart was so full of love for my mother in heaven and understood already what my head could not yet know: Mary would bring me to Jesus. The growing would be toward Jesus, for Jesus, with Jesus. Through Mary, Jesus was brought to you and to me. She was delivered up like an innocent, perfect spring flower to lighten our spirits, complete our senses, bring the very aroma of heaven to our world in need of warming, and welcome our hearts into the eternal mystery of spring and growing things.

22

The *Anima Christi,* Soul of Christ

Soul of Christ, sanctify me.
Body of Christ, come and save me.
Blood from your side, come and bathe me.
Wash me in the water of life.
Passion of Christ, strengthen and protect me.
Listen to my cry, hear and answer me.
Deep in Thy Wounds, hide and shelter me.
Wash me in the water of life.
Guard and defend me, from the foe malign.
In death's dread moments, make me only thine.
Call me and bid me, come to thee on high.
When I may praise thee with thy saints forever
and ever, Amen.

—*Lyrical adaptation by Byron Hagan*

THIS IS MY FAVORITE PRAYER. Though I saw it on the back page of many missals over the years, I did not begin to pray it, to take it to heart, until I was well into my twenties.

There remains some debate as to its authorship, but we know the prayer itself dates back to at least the fourteenth century and possibly several centuries earlier. It was a favorite of St. Ignatius of Loyola (1491–1556), who included the prayer in his popular writing *The Spiritual Exercises,* referring to it in such a way as to suggest that it was widely known even then. One of the traditions that remain around the Anima Christi prayer is to recite it silently following Holy Communion when we are meditating on the sacrament we've just received in Christ's body and blood. While I began praying the Anima Christi in this traditional fashion, it quickly grew to become the central hope for my life. The song "Anima Christi," whose lyrical adaptation is reprinted here, even became the centerpiece of my second album, also called *Anima Christi.*

It is not inaccurate to say that the "soul of Christ" found me at a time when I was crippled by fear. Various events and life circumstances, including sexual assault and illness, had virtually paralyzed me. I needed saving; I needed spiritual rescue. I had a deep longing for restoration, for the opportunity to start over, to be washed completely clean of despair. Like so many daily blessings from that painful and important time, the prayer reached out from the page and offered me loving embrace. It drew me close to the heart of Jesus—in fact, into the very mystery of Christ's sacrificial love, which makes it possible for him to heal us, restore us, and shelter us as his own.

During this time I was going to daily Mass, and I also recently had discovered a version of the rosary called the Rosary of the Holy Wounds. (For more on this, see chapter 28, "The Rosary of the Holy Wounds and Sr. Mary Martha Chambon.") Like praying the Rosary of the Holy Wounds, praying the Anima Christi brought me comfort. Its longing, almost weeping tone seemed to match the intense groaning of my own spirit. I could not have told you what it meant to pray, "Sanctify me." I felt about as far from holy as a person could get. But I found enormous comfort in the thought that I could be hidden in Christ's wounds—that I could find shelter in him. I didn't understand it and in fact found it almost macabre in some respects, but still the Holy Spirit pressed me deeper into the holy wounds of Jesus, and I was continually surprised to find ever more healing and joy.

And protection. I still need saving; I still need spiritual rescue. Jesus, the soul of Christ, is the answer to that prayer that begs for the rescue of our souls.

The church teaches that *soul* refers to "the innermost aspect of man, that which is of greatest value in him, that by which he is most especially in God's image" (*Catechism*, 363). It is in the soul where we are most like our Creator. It is his soul that we call upon to save our own, to strengthen and sanctify our own. All power, all goodness, all strength and virtue found in the human soul originates from the soul of Christ.

Indeed, the Father called me, soul to soul, his beloved daughter. He hid and healed me in his wounds. In his precious, holy wounds, he hides and heals me still. I will praise him forever.

23

ADORATION

....

THERE EXISTS A TRIBE IN a remote part of Africa that still lives fairly cloistered from the outside world. I was intrigued to learn from a sociologist who had lived among them that the English translation of their typical greeting is "I see you," to which the other person replies, "I am here." This is an epitome of my experience at adoration. We come to spend time with Jesus, who bares himself, brings himself completely to us. We come to experience more and more of him. His response is mercifully, perpetually, "I am here."

Catholics believe that Jesus is truly present in the Eucharist. (For more on this, see chapter 31, "The Eucharist.") When we speak of Eucharistic adoration, we are referring to the action of visiting Jesus in the Host, traditionally for one hour, while it is exposed, or revealed, outside the tabernacle in a monstrance. Most people use this time to pray, to talk to God, to meditate or contemplate. Or they may simply sit in the silent presence of Jesus.

It is largely our belief in the real presence that distinguishes Roman Catholics from other Christians.

Fr. Benedict Groeschel wrote in his lively book *In the Presence of Our Lord: The History, Theology, and Psychology of Eucharistic Devotion* (coauthored by James Monti):

> This mystery lights up the whole earth and sky. It sanctifies places far away from where the sacrament is reserved. . . . And this I think is what the whole Eucharistic Presence of Jesus of Nazareth is about. It doesn't need to be defended, or even explained very much. The presence of Jesus the Christ needs only to be experienced.

Few would argue that it is better to talk to loved ones on the phone than to be in their presence. Imagine truly allowing yourself to see and be seen, to be present to another person. This is an extraordinary act of intimacy, trust, and love, requiring strength and a willingness to be vulnerable. This act is encapsulated in the real presence, that eternal response of Jesus to his beloved children: "I am here." A child who has awakened from a bad dream and calls, "Momma, Momma!" doesn't want a picture of Momma, or words that remind him of Momma, though these things might help; he wants the real thing, her embrace and voice and warmth: her *presence*. And in her love and concern, she rushes to the child's bedside to say, "I'm here." Her voice calling down the hall is reassuring to the child, but it is her presence that actually facilitates his transition from feeling afraid to feeling secure and loved.

It is the same with Jesus in the tabernacle, revealed to us in adoration. It is his presence that facilitates our transition from fear to love, from confusion to peace, from death to life. What extraordinary generosity and love on the part of heaven to set things up in this way, by establishing the real presence. And how foolish we are to ignore this heavenly provision.

We are starving to be seen, to be known. Turn your TV to any "reality show" and observe our desperation on parade. Our culture preys on this basic human need. We all have it, but it cannot be filled with pixels and video and "live cams." These things only result in the loss of privacy, not in the finding of love and connection. No, these virtual substitutes are not enough. We long for the real deal.

Fr. Jeff Vonlehmen offers a poignant illustration in his book *Living Eucharist* of a father who makes long treks requiring significant sacrifice in order to attend his son's college basketball games. Fr. Vonlehmen notes: "Perhaps it would be enough to tell his son over the phone that he is thinking about him and cheering and praying for him. But think how much more it means to the child that his father is not just there in spirit—he is there in the flesh. He is providing a real presence for his son. What a big difference!"

I think of my own father, who attended countless volleyball games, art shows, and concerts, even flying once to Wichita (and it was neither convenient nor inexpensive to fly to Wichita at the time) to see me sing in a college concert. I will never forget the moment he walked into the auditorium during sound check. I shrieked from the stage and ran down to greet him. It made a huge difference to me that he was there—in spirit *and* in person.

So great is our need for this "in person" difference that entire religious orders are devoted to practicing perpetual adoration. I first discovered adoration for myself as an adult when I lived in Alaska. There was an order of cloistered nuns in the center of Anchorage at the foot of the Chugach Mountains called the Sisters of Perpetual Adoration. That anything exists in perpetuity has always been a great comfort to me. It takes my breath away still that perpetual adoration, a true prayer without ceasing, endures in sacred spaces all over the world.

The sisters' chapel was particularly appealing because of its design. A large screen separated the chapel into the public and cloistered portions of the tabernacle. On one half were the sisters. On the public half, floor-to-ceiling windows looked out over dramatic pines and mountains in the distance. The monstrance hung from the wall behind the altar and was made of green marble several feet in circumference. Twenty-four hours a day, at least one of the sisters kept Jesus company in that lovely little chapel. To be in the presence of such devoted hearts at adoration was one of the greatest privileges of my life, and I will always be grateful to those quiet, private sisters who allowed me to witness their vow of silence and simplicity.

It's not that I do not feel God's presence elsewhere. I do, in abundance. On my favorite perch on the coast of Maine. Whenever I sing or ride my bike. Riding horses, and often in the presence of children, especially my youngest nieces and nephews. It is that reassuring voice of Momma in the hallway just outside my door.

Adoration is that miraculous time when the door is thrown open and Jesus walks right in, arms wide to embrace me, and says, "My child, I am here."

The *Catechism* says that adoration is the first attitude of man, going to places beyond words, beyond noise. The beauty of greeting Jesus in adoration is that the greeting goes both ways, like an embrace. Jesus is the author of all, the beginning and end, the Alpha and Omega. He is also the source of our longing to meet him and spend time with him.

We enter his presence to hear, "My child, I see you."

"I am here, my Jesus. You called and I have come, unworthy and wanting to see you."

"I see you, and I am here," he replies, forever, for all. In this exchange lies the fantastic and sacred mystery of seeing and being seen. Knowing and being known. The source of our adoration as we leave death behind and enter into new, eternal life.

24

FASTING

....

PARDON THE IRREVERENCE, BUT ONE of the most efficacious ways to God's heart is through the stomach—*our* stomach. A priest who led a retreat I was recently on said, "If you want to know what you really want, fast. Fast with a clear intention in mind, and you'll feel clear as glass."

We cut ourselves off at the knee if we discount any of the spiritual disciplines, but I think fasting, particularly fasting accompanied by silence and increased periods of prayer and meditation, may be one of the most effective and powerful weapons we have. If you don't want to grow in God, don't fast. You'll be terribly disappointed. In fact, I find it to be such an effective spiritual discipline that I am surprised that more people don't practice it regularly, and I am very grateful to the church for continuing to encourage its practice.

But what does fasting do? Why does God expect it of us, instruct us in its execution, and bless us as a result of taking up its practice?

Fasting has long been recognized for its benefits to the body. It can be helpful to give your digestive system a rest for an extended period of time. And, because the body mirrors the spirit, when we make room in our body, we also make room in our spirit. God can more easily make himself at home in and offer direction, protection, and insight to a spirit that has made room for him. Food, like anything else, can be a distraction from hearing the voice of God. Removing food from our radar screen for a period of time facilitates our hearing the "still small voice." It is a powerful thing, too, to put your body where your mouth is, so to speak. In his booklet simply titled *Fasting*, Fr. Slavko Barbaric says it this way: "Fasting is the prayer of the whole body; it is prayer through the body. Fasting shows that our body must participate in our prayer and that our prayer must become carnal in order to become prayer in the fullest sense of the word."

There are other concrete reasons for fasting as well. Fasting reminds us of those who do not have enough to eat; it gives us perspective and builds a grateful disposition. Numerous passages in Scripture cite the importance of fasting, particularly fasting as a community. In the Old Testament, Queen Esther calls upon her people to join her in special prayer and fasting to save the lives of the Jews. Jesus clearly instructed the disciples that there were some spiritual problems that could not be healed without fasting and prayer. He fasted for forty days before entering into his public life of preaching the gospel; clearly, fasting can be a powerful tool of preparation when we are called to important work that requires special strength and utmost purity.

It's not rocket science either. There are many ways to fast: with rigor or without, alone or in concert with others for a specific intention. You can fast in preparation, as a penance, in petition or thanksgiving. If you can't fast from food, you can fast from an activity (such as watching television or movies), from socializing, or from a combination of these. And you certainly do not need to wait for Lent in order to practice this discipline. Ask God for guidance in selecting guidelines for a fast and then experiment until you find what works best for you. If all else fails, simply fast on bread and water for one day a month. Keep your fasting simple and your intention clear in your mind; then watch what happens.

Combining fasting with silence has proved to be the most powerful experience for me. During one particular three-day fast, I chose to eat only light portions of fruit and vegetables. I listened to no music, watched no television (bear in mind I was a TV junkie at the time), spoke to no one, and significantly increased my prayer and devotional time, meditating particularly on Isaiah 58, one of the most specific passages in Scripture with regard to the promises of fasting. Isaiah assures us that fasting will loose

the bonds of injustice and allow the oppressed to go free.
And it just keeps getting better:

> Your light shall break forth like the dawn,
>   and your healing shall spring up quickly;
> your vindicator shall go before you,
>   the glory of the LORD shall be your rear guard.
> Then you shall call, and the LORD will answer;
>   you shall cry for help, and he will say, Here I
>   am. . . .
> If you offer your food to the hungry
>   and satisfy the needs of the afflicted,
> then your light shall rise in the darkness
>   and your gloom be like the noonday.
> The LORD will guide you continually,
>   and satisfy your needs in parched places,
>   and make your bones strong;
> and you shall be like a watered garden,
>   like a spring of water,
>   whose waters never fail.
> Your ancient ruins shall be rebuilt;
>   you shall raise up the foundations of many
>   generations;
> you shall be called the repairer of the breach,
>   the restorer of streets to live in. (Isaiah 58:8–12)

Wow. All this for three days without television or
protein?

My stomach was groaning by the end of each day, and there were times I thought I'd die without eating something that wasn't a fruit or vegetable. There were moments when I wanted the shallow company of the droning television so badly that my eyes ached from withdrawal. Most of the time, I did not feel blissfully close to God or particularly enlightened, and my prayer often felt like a lot of work. But I offered this minor fast with the most love and earnestness I could muster. And the rewards, which came later, were very meaningful and specific to me and the intention I held in my heart throughout my fast.

The fourth day I woke up late, had an egg and a slice of toast with orange juice. I still remember how great that egg tasted.

I was not split open with insight, but I felt free as a bird. I don't know that my light broke through "like the dawn," but when I saw my best friend on the fourth day, she queried, "What have you been doing? You're glowing."

Sometimes the results of our fasts are delayed, as with any discipline that helps us grow. Sometimes we don't see the benefit in the moment, but over time we recognize the subtle shifts, the improved attitude, and the gentle freedom moving in to overtake the hardest, most imprisoned parts of our hearts.

Maybe more than anything, fasting reminds me that delay is not denial. That I have been asked to wait longer for some satisfaction, some movement, some desire to be fulfilled does not mean that God has no intention of ever fulfilling it. Fasting reminds me of the divine timetable for all things and that I am not in control of it. I can put in my requests, but ultimately God knows better than I do, and through my stomach I am reminded again and again that he has my best interests at heart.

(25)

SILENCE
....

I AM TEMPTED TO LEAVE this page blank. Filling it with words, with mental noise, would seem to defeat the purpose. But I doubt my publisher would accept this.

Silence is one of the most precious gifts I have been given through my faith. It is one of our richest traditions, practiced and cultivated by countless mystics and lay-people alike. But frankly, I owe my growing appreciation for silence to television.

One Christmas, many years ago, I gave my television away. I decided that I wanted a real Christmas, and during every holiday season my television turned into a never-ending font of ads, which grew more and more obscene by the year. Weary of my own life not looking like a credit card commercial, aware that I had the blasted box on far too often anyway, and, finally, desiring to purge these bizarre messages about the meaning of Christmas (i.e., buying stuff on sale) from my life, I unplugged the TV, loaded the thing in my Toyota, and deposited it at a friend's house. "Oh, what a feeling!"

Two weeks later—following what I confess was a brief period of rather pained withdrawal—I knew I never wanted the thing back. A peace had descended upon my house, my writing, and my life that I had not experienced for a long, long time. Perhaps never. I immediately started publishing again, my thinking became clearer, more vibrant, and I began to crave silence. St. John of the Cross, who, incidentally, never owned a television set, might have referred to it this way: "My house being now all stilled."

It was as though I had been starving myself of the very thing that would sustain and nurture me. If a child were malnourished, you wouldn't hand him a big bag of cotton candy; even if it brought a certain instant, sweet relief, its content would do far more harm than good to the child's depleted body. In the same way, the fare on television—its lack of substance and its abundance of toxic additives— was exacerbating my demise. When you add up how many hours per week the typical American watches television, it's no wonder our culture is so spiritually malnourished.

I started spending more time purposefully in silence, reading the works of the mystics who often spent lifetimes living there. To quote St. John of the Cross once more, "The Father spoke one word from all eternity and he spoke it in silence, and it is in silence that we hear it." Fr. Thomas Keating suggests that "silence is God's first language and that all other languages are poor translations." I lingered over verses like this one in Psalms: "For God alone my soul waits in silence" (62:1). Or Ecclesiastes, which speaks of "a time to keep silence, and a time to speak" (3:7). Or the Gospel of Mark: "Peace! Be still!" (4:39). Nearly all the prophets summon us to silence: "The LORD is in his holy temple; let all the earth keep silence before him!" (Habakkuk 2:20). Silence speaks to the character of God in a way that words, songs, and writing do not. It creates room for awe.

I found myself strangely aloof to the allure of advertisements that might have previously caught my attention. I left the radio off in the car and spent more time sitting quietly in the tabernacle. I learned, as Thomas Merton noted, that "the silence of the sacristy has its own sound." I started to attend silent retreat weekends and enjoyed immensely the spiritual practice of silence in the company of others. What heavenly sounds I began to hear!

So often I had complained, "God, why won't you talk to me? Why won't you answer me?" In practicing silence, I realized that the still small voice of God was always there, but I had been unwilling and unable to listen. As Robert Foster has written, "Silence is one of the deepest Disciplines of the Spirit simply because it puts the stopper on all self-justification." I had not quieted myself enough to listen because I couldn't remember what silence sounded like, and I confess I was probably deeply in love with and attached to my own words. We are a culture addicted to talking. But as St. Francis of Assisi reminds us, we are to "preach often, preach often and when necessary, use words." That posture requires a certain kind of interiority, which is cultivated in part in the spiritual discipline of silence. It is not rocket science, and it takes no American Express card to understand this.

And we need it more than ever. Our whole world has grown so noisy. As a dear friend of mine who works in the preservation of our national parks has pointed out, we are in grave danger of losing not just our forests and lakes and meadows, but also the way they *sound*.

My case, I know, is a bit extreme. I was a full-blown media junkie losing hours a day to my remote control. Even without television, my world has gone on (shocking, but true). That is not to suggest that there are not wonderful, worthy programs on television; there are. The point is that despite missing Sunday afternoon football (go Vikings!), my life has been enriched by purposefully creating quiet space for God alone to occupy in any way he wishes.

You may have distractions far graver and worthier than television: toddlers that require endless amounts of energy, a sick spouse, financial strains in a weak economy, a demanding job, emotional turmoil. But I would encourage anyone to embrace the practice of silence, to seek it with your whole heart and a willingness to listen. If you are like me, you will be surprised, delighted, and relieved to hear what you've been missing.

THE "AVE MARIA"

....

Hail Mary, full of grace, the Lord is with you.

THE WORDS WERE FIRST SPOKEN into our time and understanding by an angel. For more than two thousand years, since Gabriel's visit to Mary at the Annunciation, these words have been sung and chanted, pondered and prayed by millions, eventually reaching across every continent. They have perhaps been no more beautifully or tenderly rendered, however, than in song. Known by its Latin title, the "Ave Maria" has been the subject for numerous composers—Gounod, Bach, Verdi, and Schubert among the most famous of these—and it may be one of the most recognizable and beloved songs heaven has ever brought to earth, capturing within it the most poignant moment in all of human history.

The prayer that inspires the song, known as the Hail Mary, has had a long and interesting evolution. Marian devotions likely developed from the earliest days of the church. The first Marian prayer that we know of, "Sub Tuum Praesidium," was written in Egypt in the third century. One translation reads: "Under your mercy we take refuge, O Mother of God. Do not reject our supplications in necessity, but deliver us from danger, [O you] alone pure and alone blessed." This prayer clearly indicates that even by this time, Mary had been recognized for specific roles in the church: intercessor, human mother of the divine Jesus, and the person solely appointed to carry Christ.

Over time, the Hail Mary developed and was eventually added to the Roman Breviary, along with the Our Father, in 1568:

> *Ave Maria, gratia plena,*
> *dominus tecum,*
> *Benedicta tu in mulieribus,*
> *et benedictus fructus ventris tui, Jesus.*
> *Sancta Maria, mater Dei,*
> *ora pro nobis peccatoribus,*
> *nunc et in hora mortis nostrae. Amen.*

> Hail Mary, full of grace,
> the Lord is with you.
> Blessed are you among women,
> and blessed is the fruit of your womb, Jesus.
> Holy Mary, Mother of God,
> pray for us sinners,
> now and at the hour of our death. Amen.

Before the induction of the Hail Mary into the Breviary, music was also written in honor of Mary. We find her venerated in Gregorian chant and in other music written for or by monks at least as early as the thirteenth century.

With the angelic salutation "Greetings, favored one! The Lord is with you" (Luke 1:28), we meet Mary for the first time in Luke's Gospel. These words reverberate through history like no others. Why do they cling to our hearts, call out to be sung, and hang in the air like an ancient perfume, heavy with meaning and intoxicating to the spirit?

These words announced the Incarnation, "the word made flesh." When Gabriel paid Mary a visit and she said, "Let it be with me according to your word," God entered human history in a unique way, an unrepeatable way. He pierced the narrative of humanity, his very work of creation, to bring us his most intimate and precious gift, the most important message of all time: Jesus, Emmanuel, God with us.

The power of the "Ave Maria" is not only in the various beauties of phrasing and tension and release or the musical mechanisms and performances that raise the song to the level of fine art; the power is in the message. The message transcends even the beauty managed by Bach, Verdi, and all the others. And that message was first received, accepted, and celebrated by Mary: young, anonymous, chosen, simple. Her response was not "You're nuts!" "No thanks," or "No way; find yourself another girl." Instead, she innocently asked one question: "How?" Gabriel explained that the Holy Spirit would descend upon her, and this satisfied the young and tender heart of Mary: "Let it be with me according to your word."

For all the criticism Mary and Marian devotion take from those outside the church and even those within it, it seems brilliantly clear to me that the meaning of her life was to accept Jesus and then bring him to the world. Is our vocation really so very different?

It is different in the sense that the Holy Spirit will not visit me in the same way for the same purpose. That work, carrying Jesus, was work for which only Mary was prepared, and it has been completed. But it isn't so different in the sense that my vocation, my purpose in life, is to love Jesus, to care for him as best I can in the ways he is birthed into my life, and then to share him with the world around me.

The angel addressed her, "Hail Mary, full of grace, the Lord is with you." *Ave Maria, gratia plena. Dominus tecum.*

And this greeting is for me too. Jesus is with me too. And so too am I blessed, called, and prepared for the work of my life. So too have I been chosen by my heavenly beloved.

Pray for us, Momma—oh, how we need your prayers— now and at the hour of our death. Amen.

FORGIVENESS AND THE
SACRAMENT OF CONFESSION

As far as the east is from the west,
so far he removes our transgressions from us.
As a father has compassion for his children,
so the LORD has compassion for those
who fear him.
—Psalm 103:12–13

I DON'T KNOW IF THIS story is true, but the sentiment surely is, so I'll retell it here.

There was a little boy, uneducated and poor, who started having visions of Jesus. The boy claimed that Jesus came and spoke to him in a field. Eventually the little boy was taken before the local bishop, who questioned the authenticity of the boy's visions. The bishop instructed the boy in this way: "If you're really seeing Jesus, I want you to ask him the next time you see him, 'What was the last sin the bishop confessed?'" The little boy went off and did as he was instructed. He returned to the bishop after the next vision and said, "I did as you asked. I asked Jesus, 'What was the last sin the bishop confessed?'" "And what did he tell you?" asked the bishop. The boy replied, "He doesn't remember."

As far as the east is from the west.

Catholics sometimes take a beating for our beliefs about making confession, but consider how extraordinarily merciful Jesus was to institute this sacrament and to so generously offer us his forgiveness through another living, present being—the confessor, the priest. Jesus said to Peter, "You are Peter, and on this rock I will build my church, and the gates of Hades will not prevail against it. I will give you the keys of the kingdom of heaven, and whatever you bind on earth will be bound in heaven, and whatever you loose on earth will be loosed in heaven" (Matthew 16:18–19). Scripture says that Jesus gave his apostles "the ministry of reconciliation; that is, in Christ God was reconciling the world to himself, not counting their trespasses against them, and entrusting the message of reconciliation to us" (2 Corinthians 5:18–19). The church logically teaches that "reconciliation with God is thus the purpose and effect of this sacrament" (*Catechism,* 1468).

God forgives. Okay. But why don't I always *feel* forgiven? What makes me want to cling to my guilt?

The confessional that I visit in my local church has a large print of Rembrandt's *Return of the Prodigal Son.* The painting highlights the portion of the story where the son, starving and filthy and broken, is kneeling at the feet of his father, who welcomes him home. Imagine the depth of his love for his son! In hubris and folly, the son squandered his inheritance. And here is his father, rejoicing at his return. This was not what the son expected. He did not return home because he anticipated this sort of welcome. So why did he return? Hunger and humiliation? What was it really that prompted his return to his father and made him willing, once and for all, to give up his guilt?

In *The Return of the Prodigal Son: A Story of Homecoming,* Henri Nouwen writes:

> Do I truly want to be so totally forgiven that a
> completely new way of living becomes possible?
> Do I trust myself and such a radical reclamation?
> Do I want to break away from my deep-rooted
> rebellion that a new person can emerge? Receiving
> forgiveness requires a total willingness to let God
> be God and do all the healing, restoring, and
> renewing. As long as I want to do even a part of
> that myself, I end up with partial solutions, such
> as becoming a hired servant. As a hired servant,
> I can still keep my distance, still revolt, reject,
> strike, run away, or complain about my pay. As the
> beloved son, I have to claim my full dignity and
> begin preparing myself to become the father.

That's humbling stuff. Receiving forgiveness requires that I let go of all control and open my arms to embrace the deep responsibility that comes with being a child of God. At some point in this whole process, it may also require me to forgive myself. It is fruitful for me to remember that when I am tempted to tally my sins on the guilt scorecard, Jesus isn't keeping score at all. *As far as the east is from the west.*

The act of repentance is first an act of God's grace. It is the touch of God on our lives that allows us to surrender and be naked before him. We come out of hiding and are *protected* in his presence. We come at our most vulnerable, our most ashamed, and are embraced. We are prodigal son to the compassionate Father, who rejoices at our return.

Still, receiving forgiveness means that I am going to be restored to dignity. I won't be rolling around with the pigs in the mud anymore, and maybe I liked that just a bit, the selfishness and irresponsibility of sin. Instead, I must "begin preparing myself" to grow and to forgive as I have been forgiven. That sounds like *work.*

See how God ties fatherhood and sonship together; you can't have one without the other. They depend on one another. So too, it is important to remember that following Jesus means that we ask forgiveness *and* we forgive; we take up our cross *and* we get help in carrying it. Just as the Lord's Prayer links forgiveness and forgiving—"Forgive us our trespasses as we forgive those who trespass against us"—so must we. Of course, that's not always easy either.

The *Catechism* says it so plainly:

> Now—and this is daunting—this outpouring
> of mercy cannot penetrate our hearts as long as
> we have not forgiven those who have trespassed

against us. Love, like the Body of Christ, is indivisible; we cannot love the God we cannot see if we do not love the brother or sister we do see. In refusing to forgive our brothers and sisters, our hearts are closed and their hardness makes them impervious to the Father's merciful love; but in confessing our sins, our hearts are opened to his grace. (2840)

God's forgiveness doesn't make sense; it doesn't add up to a logical, proven equation. It's much better than that, and this may be where so many of us go astray. It seems too good to be true that God would not withdraw his love from us when we act badly, when we commit sin. If you find yourself struggling with confession or forgiveness, either receiving it or offering it, you're certainly not alone. It is a big lesson, one we all probably learn over the course of a lifetime.

As you struggle, remember too that "forgiveness also bears witness that, in our world, love is stronger than sin" (*Catechism*, 2844). There is forgiveness out there for you, just as for everyone else, to be given and received. *As far as the east is from the west.* We need only get honest, get on our knees, and let God be God.

Father, mercy.

28

THE ROSARY OF THE HOLY WOUNDS AND SR. MARY MARTHA CHAMBON

THE ROSARY OF THE HOLY Wounds is one of the many variations on the traditional rosary (see chapter 4, "The Rosary"). This devotion was revealed to Bd. Sr. Mary Martha Chambon, who lived in France from 1841 to 1907. The five decades of the rosary beads correspond nicely with the five holy wounds, and I find it powerful to pray this devotion with my favorite crucifix in my lap.

On the crucifix and the first three beads, you recite:

Jesus, Divine Redeemer, be merciful to us and to the whole world. Amen.

Strong God, holy God, immortal God, have mercy on us and on the whole world. Amen.

Grace and mercy, O my Jesus, during present dangers; cover us with Your Precious Blood. Amen.

Eternal Father, grant us mercy through the Blood
of Jesus Christ, Your only Son; grant us mercy,
we beseech You. Amen, Amen, Amen.

The following prayers you recite using the rest of the rosary beads.

Leader Eternal Father, I offer You the Wounds of
our Lord Jesus Christ.
Response To heal the wounds of our souls.

On the small beads:

L. My Jesus, pardon and mercy.
R. Through the merits of Your Holy Wounds.

My first reaction to this devotion mirrored my discomfort with the sorrowful mysteries of the traditional rosary. Did we really have to linger over wounds? Wasn't that morbid or sick in some way? Didn't it draw an unnatural or exaggerated feeling of guilt from the emotional part of our psyche? How would such emotionalism benefit my spiritual life? The idea of meditating on Christ's wounds reminded me of people who slow down while driving past car crashes, straining for a view of the victims trapped in mangled steel. How would this help me grow in love?

Still, it was short and it was simple. This devotion was faster than the rosary and seemed to require less concentration—more *intention* than *attention.* In the beginning, I didn't have much more to offer to meditation than my intention to try to practice it. Refining my attention seemed too painful and improbable. But as my practice of the devotion grew, so did my attraction to the meditation. In fact, it became so strong that I found I couldn't wait to finish the traditional rosary in order to get to the "really satisfying" prayer of the Holy Wounds meditation. So what happened?

First, I considered the source of this devotion. Sr. Mary Martha's life was simple. She was a cloistered nun living in the Monastery of the Visitation of Chambéry. Jesus revealed the practice and promises of this devotion to her while she was in deep prayer, and she recorded the experience. There was simplicity in the account, no melodrama, and there certainly wasn't anything in it for Sr. Mary Martha. She was cloistered, after all, and died in the odor of sanctity (a phenonmenon associated with saints and extremely holy people, like Padre Pio, who bore an unusually sweet smell which could be attributed to no external substance like perfume or powder), and the cause for her beatification was introduced in 1937—all of which made her experience credible and notable.

Second, I considered the promises of the devotion themselves. They are somewhat lengthy, and I recommend you read them in their fullness, as Bd. Sr. Mary Martha recorded them (see appendix). At first, in my healthy skepticism, I thought that these "promises" might just be saintly hocus-pocus meant only for "religious types" like Bd. Sr. Mary Martha, surely not for someone living in the real world. Still, as I read them, over and over, by and large they promised the one thing I really wanted: *healing.*

> My Wounds will repair yours. My wounds will cover all your faults. . . . In meditation on them, you will always find a new love. . . . Plunge your actions into My Wounds and they will be of value. . . . When you have some trouble, something to suffer, quickly place it in My Wounds, and the pain will be alleviated.

At the time I discovered this devotion, I felt wounded. Let me be clear: not bruised, not depressed, not down—*wounded,* mortally so. Now there was overreaction, exaggeration of my hurts, and self-pity to wade through, but those problems were also part of the woundedness, a part I came to believe God was aggressively interested in removing. So I clung to those promises with all my strength, long before they began to manifest themselves.

Now this devotion begins my day. The prayers of the Rosary of the Holy Wounds have come to live with me in a way that no other prayers have. I say them automatically when I walk up to receive communion, when I find myself with a free minute, when I swim laps, or when I jog along the Charles River. "My Jesus, pardon and mercy" fills my mind when I am standing in line at the movie theater or the grocery store, when I'm waiting for my roommate to get out of the shower, and often throughout the day for no particular reason at all.

Lest you think I'm laying out my piety for all to admire, I will add that Bd. Sr. Mary Martha also recorded, "You can always purify yourself in My Wounds." There has been no more efficacious meditation for me than this to work through the obstacles that keep me from being close to God. Fear, self-pity, selfishness, low self-esteem, arrogance, pride, resentment: these are the wounds that truly cripple, that truly, mortally wound the spirit. Through this devotion, I have found great and ongoing relief for them—mighty holy repair.

Though I no longer feel so raw, I still bear scars, as we all do. There are circumstances that open the wounds again from time to time, but I plunge them into his wounds, and the pain is alleviated in many forms. God doesn't always remove the pain but instead gives "the wound" a purpose I did not expect, or gives me insight into a problem. Sometimes God might strengthen me with graces and virtues I didn't even know I lacked. I am learning that we carry our wounds for a lifetime, but through grace, we're on our way to resurrection and restoration. We're on our way to "a new love," one that promises repair, purity, mercy, and healing.

My Jesus, pardon and mercy for all your children through the merits of Your Holy Wounds.

For Fr. Zlatko Sudac

29

PILGRIMAGES

....

WE ARE A PEOPLE SEEKING, a people longing to be found. Pilgrimages are an answer to that inner urge, a holy invitation to "come and see." As María Ruiz Scaperlanda writes so beautifully in *The Journey: A Guide for the Modern Pilgrim,* the book she coauthored with her husband, Michael, we "come and touch the hand of God" as pilgrims. "A person doesn't pick the place. The place picks the person and invites her to come, be still, and know God in a new and unpredictable way." This is really the heart and soul of any pilgrimage, no matter one's religion; it's also the heart and soul of the journey we all take as God's children.

Mass is my daily pilgrimage. Every noon hour, I leave my office—the phone, the fax, the computer, my e-mail. I walk down Mt. Auburn Street through Harvard Square, over the brick sidewalks past Peet's Coffee and the 7-Eleven and the historic Adams House, where Franklin Roosevelt lived when he was an undergraduate, to St. Paul's Roman

Catholic Church, located at the ironic intersection of Bow and Arrow streets. I move through the bustle of students and tourists and street vendors, carrying nothing except my rosary and maybe a notebook if I plan to stay for a while afterward to write. My body does the work, step after step, carrying with it my heart and my mind, and I place them all, along with my desires and hopes and disappointments and plans, on the altar with Jesus.

You call, Lord; I answer your bidding; do with me what you will.

I contemplate the reading, receive the Body and Blood, receive the final blessing, pay a visit to the tabernacle, and then make the return trip back to my office.

It was not a conscious decision on my part to start attending Mass daily. I only know that I started to feel a gentle pull and a kind of sweet gnawing if I didn't attend frequently. Some pilgrimages sneak up on us like that and become a part of our daily lives, our daily surrender to the invitation, "Come and follow me." Others call us more dramatically, and we might travel far from home and familiar things, across oceans and mountains and plains, along uncertain paths. The trip might be far more arduous than navigating Harvard Square during a busy noon hour. In any case, it is vitally important that we listen to and answer that urge to visit sacred spaces and places.

During the Jubilee Year, I had the great opportunity to work as a volunteer at the Vatican, along with other volunteers from around the world. That two months in Rome was the longest, most challenging pilgrimage I've ever taken.

Most of the English-speaking volunteers were housed in an apartment complex about one hour from the center of Rome in Torre Maura. During my stay, I had two roommates who did not speak English: Marisa from Spain and Dolores from Venezuela. Each morning, our assignments for the day were posted on a sheet at the front desk. You never knew where you were supposed to show up for work until that morning. It could be any one of a dozen or more pilgrimage sites: Divine Amore, outside Rome; St. John Lateran, St. Paul's Outside the Wall, the Basilica of St. Mary Major, St. Peter's Basilica, the Catacombs; the Colosseum; or somewhere else.

You didn't know what time you were to arrive until that morning either. You might have a morning, afternoon, or evening shift. There might be directions to where you were to meet, or you might have to wing it. Once you arrived at your destination—by foot, by train, by bus, or by some combination of all three—it might not be clear exactly what your work was that day. Sometimes you were assigned with other English speakers, and sometimes you weren't. Sometimes you could travel in a group. Other times, you were on your own. Occasionally the buses arrived on schedule; more often it was anyone's guess. All in all, it was very much a "fly by the seat of your pants" kind of experience. You were in for a lot of aggravation if you were the kind of person who required planning and predictability.

But in the unknowing, the uncertainty, the disorganization (an endearing Italian penchant), you were forced to surrender to the whim and whimsy of the Holy Spirit. You couldn't plan, you couldn't predict, you couldn't control anything; the Scaperlandas might agree that this loss of all control is essential to growing a pilgrim heart.

Pilgrimages are a wonderful means of reminding us of our humanity, our weaknesses, and our most basic desires and needs. Thomas à Kempis wrote that "the time of adversity shows who is of most virtue. Occasions do not make a man frail, but they do show openly what he is." The same is true of pilgrimages. Like so many millions of people that year, I had come to walk through the holy doors of all the designated basilicas, to visit holy places in the hopes of bringing some of that holiness home with me. I came burdened with petitions for myself and my family and lightened by gratitude for so many blessings already received. Before my time in Italy, I used to think of myself as a pretty easygoing, flexible person. But I have to confess, I didn't feel all that holy or easygoing through much of it. Mainly this pilgrim felt annoyed, frightened, and exhausted. Sometimes it was the other volunteers—this one was too controlling, that one too talkative. Or I was bothered by the constant demands of other pilgrims and tourists: "No, the Sistine Chapel is NOT in St. Peter's Basilica, and YES, you must check your backpacks at the *guardaroba* despite your protests that you carry no pope-threatening materials."

The young *capos*, or managers who supervised us, could be apathetic and dismissive. My ID badge mistakenly said that I was fluent not just in English and Italian, but in French and German as well. When my gross ignorance (in all four languages!) was discovered each day, they often gave me the most tedious postings. Each day it was a new *capo* and a new humiliation at being a "dumb American."

There were the taxi drivers who tried to take you for a "ride," and the pickpockets who tried to steal your wallet. It was cold and rainy some days, and you'd have to stand for hours and hours on the hard cobblestone streets getting soaked while giving directions to the medic, to La Cappella Sistina, to the subway, to the Spanish Steps, to the ATM, to the bank, to the bathroom.

Oh, there were so many days when I did not like what my circumstances revealed of my character, or lack thereof. It was painful to see myself so clearly, without the usual mechanisms and conveniences I was accustomed to using to cover up my impatience, immaturity, pettiness, and self-absorption.

It is a merciful act of God to allow us to see ourselves as we are. Until we do, we cannot grow. Pilgrimages help us move through obstacles and our own weaknesses to discover not just what lies on the exterior landscape, but also what frontiers within us need to be uncovered, discovered, mined, and made ready and useful for the long journey home to heaven.

We are all traveling toward something. We go out and come back, and the journey has changed us, has opened our eyes to new interior, spiritual landscapes by taking us to new lands. "Where we are is where we've come from," writes Fr. Murray Bodo, "transformed by way of arriving." Whether on pilgrimage through Harvard Square, the Piazza Navona, or someplace else, we find Jesus ready to keep us close company there and back again.

HOUSE BLESSINGS

....

Home interprets heaven.
Home is heaven for beginners.
—Charles H. Parkhurst

I**N MY THIRTY-SEVEN YEARS**, I have moved numerous times and, as a result, have become quite an aficionado of the art of house blessings. If nothing else, house blessings are always a good excuse to throw a party.

My most recent house blessing consisted of an open house and a formal blessing at 3:00 PM, the Hour of Divine Mercy. Friends gathered in my new home, and we took turns reading passages from my priest's huge book of beautiful blessings:

> The Son of God, Lord of heaven and earth, made
> his home among us. With thankfulness and
> gladness let us call upon him.

> Lord Jesus Christ, by your life with Mary and
> Joseph you sanctified the life of the home; dwell

with us in our home, so that we may have you as
our guest and honor you as our Head.

In you every dwelling grows into a holy temple;
grant that those who live in this house may be
built up together into the dwelling place of God in
the Holy Spirit.

You taught your followers to build their houses
upon solid rock; grant that the members of this
family may hold fast to your teachings and, free of
all discord, serve you with their whole heart.

You had no place to lay your head, but in
uncomplaining poverty you accepted the
hospitality of your friends; grant that through our
help people who are homeless may obtain decent
housing.

We passed the book around and read several passages
from Luke—Martha welcoming Jesus into her home; Jesus
promising Zacchaeus, "Today salvation has come to this
house" (Luke 10:38; 19:9). When we were through, Father
raised his hands and, making the sign of the cross, gave the
house a good dousing with holy water. (He also managed to
douse a few of my friends, some of whom were not Catholic
and were a little surprised to be splashed with holy water at
three in the afternoon on a Sunday in my living room.)

The house blessing is a tradition that we don't embrace as much as we used to. I remember occasional "house blessing days" when I was a kid, when our parish priest would drive around with holy water and sprinkle it on the lawns and front doors of the homes of his parishioners. He'd say a short, sweet prayer at each stop, asking for blessing and protection on the families that dwelled there, and then move on to the next house. A drive-by blessing.

As an adult, I first asked my priest to bless my house because I was working at home, trying to get published, and because I was starving, I was willing to accept help from any potential source. As I have grown older, home has become a more profound place in my life. To be "at home" means more than it used to; it carries more weight—it means safety, living comfortably in my own skin. And blessing my home is a visible action that invites God into the most important, most intimate aspects of my life, the places that matter the most to me, the places where I really live, work, worship, and try to learn how to love.

I have my house blessed because I want to invite God in, really. I want God to inhabit every part of my life, from my writing space to my sleeping space, in the nooks and crannies where dust sometimes collects, and in the spaces that I share with my housemate. I don't want to invite God to visit after I've given the place a thorough scrubbing. I want to invite God to move in, to live here with me. This is how we make home "heaven for beginners," by continually inviting God to dwell with us in the most intimate chambers of our souls and by asking his help as we learn how to love those who are closest to us, who fill our homes and daily lives with their love and imperfections, their presence, needs, personalities, and opinions.

How wonderful it would be to get to heaven and find that we recognize the place, that it is already familiar, home. Parkhurst was on to something when he wrote, "Home interprets heaven. Home is heaven for beginners." It reminds me that God is interested in establishing the heavenly kingdom right here, right now, within me. My life now is a practice run for life eternal. I don't know about you, but I welcome the opportunity for far more practice.

Jesus, do not be my guest, but make your home with me.

31

THE EUCHARIST

....

THERE WERE YEARS I WANDERED around exploring other expressions of faith, other churches, and other ways of taking up the spiritual life. I don't regret them; God is merciful, and I learned while wandering. But eventually I missed aspects of the church that could not be replaced elsewhere, namely, the sacraments. More than all others, I missed Holy Communion, or the Eucharist. There is simply no substitute for the real presence of Jesus.

If you earnestly wonder about the Mass, I recommend first that you actually *go* to Mass. You can read about it all you like, but the experience of it is the better teacher. Go, ask the Holy Spirit to open your heart and ears and eyes, and then trust what comes. That said, it is important to offer a brief history of its development. How did the church get from the Last Supper to the sacrifice of the Mass celebrated in your local parish on Sunday? It wasn't so long a trip.

Jesus instituted two sacraments at the Last Supper: the Eucharist and the priesthood. The Eucharist makes it possible for all generations of believers to participate in His Passion and to experience salvation; the priesthood carries the Eucharist to the community of believers. With his chosen ones gathered together, Jesus gave thanks, broke the bread, and said, "This is my body, which is given for you." Then he did the same with the cup, saying, "Do this in remembrance of me." Because I am his chosen one as well, there is a seat for me at the table, too. I do what he said, and I remember. I am filled with profound gratitude that I am not limited to simply reading about Christ's works and actions that make it possible for me to be reunited with God. God loves me so much that he makes certain I experience it firsthand.

Church history tells us that the present structure of the Mass has been handed down for centuries. A complete account of this can be found in the explanation that St. Justin Martyr offered to the pagan emperor Antoninus Pius around the year 155 (*Catechism*, 1345) In brief, the Mass consists of believers who gather together to celebrate the Liturgy of the Word, reading passages from the Old Testament, the New Testament, and the Gospels, followed by a presentation of offerings and the prayer of consecration. It is at this point that the same Holy Spirit who visited Mary during the Annunciation descends upon the gifts and changes them from bread and wine to Body and Blood. This is called transubstantiation.

This Eucharistic prayer, also called the anaphora, is breathtaking and complete in its appointments. Flannery O'Connor called the liturgy "beautifully flat." Next time you go to Mass, really listen to it. As the *Catechism* recalls, it is in the Eucharistic prayer that "we come to the heart and summit of the celebration. . . . [The] power of the words and the action of Christ, and the power of the Holy Spirit, make sacramentally present under the species of bread and wine Christ's body and blood, his sacrifice offered on the cross once for all" (1352–53).

Once for all. These are important words. The sacrifice of the Mass is not an additional sacrifice. Christ is not dying over and over. It is the same sacrifice that was offered at Calvary, offered forever. It is not magic, but it is certainly a mystery.

When Catholics speak of the real presence, they are referring to Christ's body and blood that become manifest in the bread and wine. (For more on this, see chapter 23, "Adoration.") My friend Fr. Jeff Vonlehmen describes it this way in his book, *Living Eucharist: The Transforming Presence of Christ*:

> There's no substitute for a real flesh and blood
> relationship. . . . When we hear about body and
> blood as sacrifice, as in the sacrifice of the Mass,
> we think somebody or something has been killed.
> But in the scriptural world-view, the thought
> of blood is the presence of life. Sacrifice means

communion of life. This brings to mind the
wonderful image of an infant in the mother's
womb. The infant is being nourished through
the umbilical cord by the body and blood of the
mother. It's not a violent act—the baby is receiving
life. The mother's body is making all kinds of
changes and sacrifices for the infant in her womb.
But the mother is not thinking, "Oh, my body
is making all kinds of sacrifices for the infant in
my womb." Instead, the mother is very conscious
of the communion she has with her infant, a
community of life. This relationship is truly a
body and blood relationship.

This body-and-blood relationship is the kind that Christ
wants to have with us, that he has designed us to have with
him. I am his child, his creation; he is my Father, and that
is as real to me as my relationship with my earthly mother
and father. Jesus doesn't phone in his presence, doesn't send
postcards or telegrams saying, Having a great time—wish
you were here. *He is here.* There's just no substitute for the
real thing.

There are many extraordinary scholarly works on the
Eucharist available for further study. You might begin by
reading the Gospels and the *Catechism,* and, of course, by
attending Mass, especially on a weekday, when you might
encounter fewer distractions. If it's been a while since
you've been to Mass, don't worry about the lapse; just go.

If you've never been to a Mass before in your life, find a local church and join us. You are invited. Jesus is there and willing to offer you a body-and-blood relationship that will change you forever. I promise that he has a seat for you at the banquet table of his supper, and no one can take your place. It is reserved eternally for the one and only you.

32

THE SIGN OF PEACE

....

IT IS A SIMPLE GESTURE, but it carries great weight. I wish we took more time with it and remembered what it is that we're really doing when we extend our hands to one another.

During the Mass, Catholics offer one another a sign of peace after the consecration of the Body and Blood. It is usually a handshake, maybe a hug or kiss in the case of close friends and family. Especially in the case of my brothers when we were still children, the sign of peace was often anything but peaceful—more a circuslike departure from the solemnity of the Mass. The sign of peace offered by my brothers would include a tug that would pull you off balance, or a pinch or slug, or some other such display of boyhood affection. You knew to take hold of something before extending your hand to my brother Joe.

The playfulness of my family at the sign of peace during Mass has always been a source of joy and comfort for me because, by and large, we all know that we *are* at peace with one another. Our joyfulness and playfulness is a fruit of that peace. When I was a child, the sign of peace was my favorite part of the Mass because our security in our love for, and friendship with, one another was brought so plainly to the surface. I know that I am incredibly blessed; it's not like that for everyone. But there's more to the sign of peace than expressing affection.

The sign of peace falls after the consecration and before communion as a none-too-subtle suggestion that we should be reconciled with one another and with God before receiving Jesus into our body. As much as possible, we need to be holy vessels to receive our holy God.

During the Mass, the priest repeats the words of Jesus: "My peace I leave you; my peace I give to you." The passage comes from the Gospel of St. John:

> The advocate, the Holy Spirit, whom the Father
> will send in my name, will teach you everything,
> and remind you of all that I have said to you.
> Peace I leave with you; my peace I give to you. I
> do not give to you as the world gives. Do not let
> your hearts be troubled, and do not let them be
> afraid. (John 14:26–27)

When we offer one another a sign of peace at Mass or at other times, it is the peace of Jesus, the peace he left us, that we extend to one another. As I grow in faith, I have come to understand that the presence of peace is not necessarily the absence of hardship or heartache or even chaos. In fact, the very presence of interior peace may be an indicator that a person is surrounded by circumstances that are anything but peaceful.

Peace is a fruit of the Holy Spirit and a manifestation of the presence of God. Fr. Canon Francis Ripley defines it as "the state of a soul that is at rest with God, with others and with oneself." True rest, true peace, is a state of my interior not necessarily reflected on the exterior, and it requires some work and commitment on my part. Being at rest with God means I am, to the best of my human knowledge and ability, hiding nothing from God. Nothing do I keep from him, not even my resentments and shortcomings and weaknesses. I come before him with all that I am. To the best of my human ability, I have no resentments with others either. If I need to ask forgiveness, I do. If I need to confront someone about a wrong committed against me, I do. If I need to forgive, I do. Peace is most certainly not the absence of difficulty, but the Gospel assures me that the peace of Jesus can live at the center of me even in the midst of trial. "I have said this to you," says Jesus, "so that in me you may have peace. In the world you face persecution. But take courage; I have conquered the world!" (John 16:33).

So how, you may wonder, can peace coexist with this promise of persecution? Isn't this a contradictory notion? If

God's presence brings peace, how can persecution or trial continue? Wouldn't it be eradicated in the presence of the Almighty?

It is important to understand that the peace of Jesus is offered to us freely, though it came at a price, and the price was Jesus' suffering. St. Paul's letter to the Ephesians says:

> He is our peace; in his flesh he has made [us] into one and has broken down the dividing wall, that is, the hostility between us. He has abolished the law with its commandments and ordinances, that he might create in himself one new humanity in place of the two, thus making peace, and might reconcile both groups to God in one body through the cross, thus putting to death that hostility through it. (2:14–16)

Peace is offered to us, made available to us through the *work* of the cross. We can be reconciled to God, to one another, and to ourselves only through the *sacrifice* of Jesus. To be givers of peace in this life, we must be willing to sacrifice. And sacrifice can be costly.

When Jesus offers us his peace, he offers us his sacrifice. When I extend my hand to another person in the sign of peace, I need to be willing to be reconciled and to sacrifice myself. It is easy for me to shake hands thinking, *I'll like you and wish you well as long as your interests do nothing to hinder my own agenda.* Anyone who grew up in a family of seven children knows that peace like that isn't really peace. Likewise, it can be costly for me to extend peace to someone who may require much from me—more tolerance than I think I am capable of, more understanding, or simply room for disagreement.

Do you know the peace of Jesus? Is this peace what moves through your mind and heart and hand when you extend your hand at Mass on Sunday? Are you willing to sacrifice yourself for peace?

As Catholics, we do not give as the world gives. We do not offer what the world offers. When we offer the sign of peace, one to another, stranger or friend, brother or sister in Christ, this is the peace we offer: the sacrificial peace of Jesus.

Peace of Jesus be with you.

PART FOUR

Truths That Bring Grace

(33)

To Arrive at Love

···

A N EDITOR TOLD ME ONCE that no one ever reads
introductions or prefaces. Since I had written an
introduction to my first book and was determined to
prove him wrong (lest he cut my precious prose, which he
most certainly did), I tallied the most significant prefaces
and prologues I remembered reading. The first to rise to
the surface of my mind was the introduction to my big,
chunky *Catechism.* In its early pages is this passage, quoted
from the Roman Catechism; in my copy it is underlined
in purple ink:

> The whole concern of doctrine and its teaching must
> be directed to the love that never ends. Whether
> something is proposed for belief, for hope or for
> action, the love of our Lord must always be made
> accessible, so that anyone can see that all the works
> of perfect Christian virtue spring from love and have
> no other objective than to arrive at love. (25)

That concludes the prologue. The rest of the book is a how-to manual, feeding us with ways and means to reach the objective: arriving at love.

For passages like this I have come to love my *Catechism* as an old and wise friend, wrinkled and tattered and full of life and inspiration, an anchor that holds even in the roughest waters of church history. It is full of the voices and personalities of our most beloved, steadfast brethren—the apostles, the prophets, St. Thomas Aquinas, St. Augustine, St. Ambrose, St. John of the Cross, all the early church fathers. The wisdom, scholarship, and experience that have shaped its pages are not only worthy of my respect, but something I desperately need as well. Flannery O'Connor once wrote in a letter to a friend that, for her, "dogma is only a gateway to contemplation and is an instrument of freedom, not restriction. It preserves mystery for the human mind." While nothing is lacking within Scripture, and we know it to be complete, I find that the study of the catechism heightens my desire to meditate on Scripture, especially the words of Jesus, bearing in mind this single purpose: *to arrive at love.*

For me, to arrive at love ultimately means to arrive at the truth of Jesus. Indeed, his love is a "mystery for the human mind." When he came, he changed all the standing rules on love, instructing us to "love your enemies and pray for those who persecute you" (Matthew 5:44). He encouraged us to set aside the worries of the day and to "instead, strive for [God's] kingdom" (Luke 12:31), a kingdom with the single purpose of loving God and one another. St. Paul said it this way: if we do not have love, we are nothing, a "noisy gong or a clanging cymbal" (1 Corinthians 13:1). If our teaching and preaching and outreach and evangelism do not spring from the desire to love, then we have missed the mark indeed. The point is not necessarily about being right but about being truthful and loving.

The death of love may be the most excruciating pain there is. We've all experienced it, in one form or another. We started a relationship with promises and hope in our heart, and then circumstances arose to choke and destroy love. Or maybe we were rejected for another and were unable to forgive or receive forgiveness. Maybe illness or some other unpredictable, insurmountable difficulty arose. For whatever reason, love came to an end. There was no more of it. Because we are human, because we have experienced this loss of love with others, it can sometimes be challenging to believe that in Jesus, love never ends.

And I certainly don't have to look to the love of others to challenge this idea. My own love runs out, grows cold, becomes fickle, and wavers under stress, fatigue, weariness. For me, the biggest, ugliest obstacle to love is fear. When love seems to run away from me, I can do myself a big favor by answering this question: Of what am I afraid?

A wise spiritual mentor once told me that his fears seemed to break down into two categories: "Am I okay?" and "What will others think?" As I examine my life, I see that these two questions drive most of my own fears too.

When I find myself falling into a fearful place, I take these two questions to God. *Abba, Father, am I okay? Lord, what will they think of me?*

How do you suppose he answers them?

I love the voices of the Old Testament prophets, powerful and present in their admonitions to cast fear aside. Fiery Isaiah is one of my favorites. He says, "Thus says the LORD, / he who created you . . . : / Do not fear, for I have redeemed you; / I have called you by name, you are mine. . . . / Because you are precious in my sight, / and honored, and I love you" (Isaiah 43:1, 4). Or St. John, who says, "God is love, and those who abide in love abide in God. . . . There is no fear in love, but perfect love casts out fear" (1 John 4:16–18). The catechism understands that so often where Scripture speaks of fear, it follows up with the antidote of love.

Jesus' voice is all the more edifying when it comes to love and fear. More than a dozen times in the New Testament, he says, "Do not be afraid. Do not fear. Do not worry." I believe that he was not so much scolding us for lacking faith as reminding us, "My love never ends. There's plenty. It doesn't run out. It can cover everything, everyone." And if the opposite of love is fear, there cannot be any fear where Jesus is. When we arrive at love, when we arrive at the truth of Jesus, we are no longer afraid.

Where do you take your fear? What do you do with it? I am in greater danger of damaging my relationship with God, others, and myself because of fear than for any other reason. I am in greater danger of missing that single purpose—to arrive at love—from the ravages that fear can bring. Fear forgets God. Fear forgets our true purpose. Fear forgets the *love that never ends*.

Of course, fear is God given at times. It can be a wonderful help, bringing saving information in moments of crisis. My spiritual director says too that "some things are scary in life because they're scary." Pain brings our body important information so that we can correct and heal ourselves. In the same way, fear brings us important information so that we can protect ourselves when appropriate. We need our rational fears to help keep us out of danger. We need a healthy "fear of the Lord," a respect for his nature, to have a right understanding of ourselves. But this *love that never ends* outlasts fear. This perfect love casts out fear. That is what I never want to forget.

It was probably a loving thing that my editor put the kibosh on my introduction. It probably wasn't that good. Maybe he saved me from looking foolish, and, I mean, really: what might people think? But I also have him to thank for reminding me that sometimes there are tender, powerful tidbits hidden in these opening paragraphs we tend to overlook. When I feel swamped with fears and insecurities, I can go back to the beginning of things and remind myself where I'm headed, and that in arriving at love I will find a love that never ends.

Remove my fears, Lord, and anything that keeps me from arriving at love.

34

HEAVENLY HUMOR

TRULY HOLY PEOPLE POSSESS a lightness of spirit, an ability to laugh at themselves. Ecclesiastes assures us that there is a "time to laugh," and Proverbs confirms that "a cheerful heart is good medicine." The Italians say it this way: *Il ros fa buon sangue,* or, literally, "Laughter makes good blood." Humor is healing. A happy, laughing heart is healthy. In the face of difficulty and disappointment, God has frequently brought me to tears, not out of pain but from laughter. What Jesus has taught me about suffering has helped me to laugh in some difficult (and some simply annoying) situations.

I first learned to find the humor in life, even in the face of great trials, from my own parents. They were both diagnosed with cancer within one month of each other, both operated on within weeks of each other. Shortly after their surgeries, they were standing in front of the mirror one morning, my father's lower torso wrapped and bandaged, my mother's upper torso wrapped and bandaged. They took turns pointing at each other, laughing, and saying, "Between the two of us, we make up about one healthy person." Rather than stewing over the loss of body parts, they were able to have some fun with it. What a wonderful example! I confess I am not always able to live up to it.

One harrowing evening comes quickly to mind. I was returning from my pilgrimage to Rome, and the trip home proved to be one of the most challenging parts of the journey. I arrived in Amsterdam at 11:30 PM only to find that the airport hotel was closed and there was no place for me to go for a fifteen-hour layover. I was out of money, out of energy for negotiating with non-English speakers, and out of ideas about what to do for the many hours of utter sleepless agony. None of the airport offices were open; neither were any restaurants or shops in the terminal. However, I managed to wander around Schiphol Airport until I found a baby-changing bathroom, complete with a lock on the door. I rolled in my suitcase, changed into my jammies after taking a kind of half bath with my washcloth, brushed my teeth, made a makeshift bed on the floor, and thought, *Well, at least I can lie down for a few hours.* I was feeling mighty smart about my terminal rescue and thanking God for his nifty provision. A journal entry at 12:02 AM reads, "Even soaked my feet a bit and so am feeling quite clever. There's nothing better than clean teeth, clean face, and clean feet." I said a prayer to Padre Pio to keep me safe and undiscovered until at least 5:00 AM.

The next entry in my journal is from 2:52 AM and begins with some expletives I will not repeat here, but the gist is that I was discovered by the cleaning crew and kicked out. "I wanted to punch these people—I had actually fallen asleep!" The cleaning crew hovered over me to make certain I left. As I was repacking my bag, I began singing "Great Is Thy Faithfulness," out of spite if nothing else. After my complete discombobulation and ousting from the baby-care room, I decided I needed to change out of my jammies. So I moseyed into the bathroom and started to change. Halfway through my change, I noticed the strangest objects on the wall. They were big circular things, like nothing I'd ever seen before, and I thought, *This is some kind of strange bidet.* Through all this, I continued to sing "Great Is Thy Faithfulness."

My task completed, I had started to put away some of my things when a man walked in. He looked at me, and I at him, and I thought, *The Dutch are liberal; this is probably a unisex restroom.* But the guy was looking a little hesitant. He eventually walked over to what I then realized were not bidets at all, but urinals.

Great is thy faithfulness, oh God our Father.

So the dude unzipped his pants.

Morning by morning new mercies I see.

He stood there for what seemed like forever, unable to go—my presence clearly impeding his process.

All I have needed Thy hand hath provided.

He finally relieved himself and left. It was only as I was walking out, still singing, that I noticed the "Herren" sign at the entrance.

So here I was, a devout Roman Catholic returning from a two-month pilgrimage in Rome singing a Baptist hymn in the men's restroom at Schiphol Airport at three in the morning in my pajamas.

Oh Lord, may I always be the picture of such holiness.

Scripture teaches us that Jesus was fully human. He wept. He got angry. He felt pain. He loved to the bitter end, and I'm absolutely convinced that being fully human also meant that he laughed. A laughing Jesus may not be the image you carry with you, but at three in the morning in the Schiphol men's room, I believe my Jesus was right there with me, and he was laughing too.

My sweet and gentle Jesus, give me a heart that laughs often and easily.

35

CELIBACY

....

THERE WILL BE THOSE WHO really don't like this
chapter (some days I'm one of them), but celibacy is
a more viable, more beautiful, and more useful lifestyle
choice than our culture would have us believe. Two dangers often arise when discussing this topic: scrupulosity
and laxity. I pray wholeheartedly to avoid them both.

Consider this for a moment: a person self-possessed
is a free person. A person self-possessed is controlled by
nothing, ruled by no one, free to choose. Ask yourself: Am
I self-possessed? What controls me? What or whom do I
serve? Am I free to choose?

Consider this too: a survey published by a Christian
magazine some years ago asked married Protestant ministers how many of them, if given the chance to do things
over, would, as ministers, remain single rather than marry
and raise a family in addition to being clergy. An overwhelming majority indicated that they would choose to
be single—not because they didn't love their wives and

children, but because they did! These ministers and their families bore the burden of often feeling divided; the families suffered as a result, often forced to be "second chair" to the needs of their congregations.

Celibacy is, first and foremost, about freeing us to live with a singleness of purpose. Unfortunately, we often perceive it simply as a choice that starves us of our natural sexual needs and desires.

The most obvious definition of celibacy is associated with religious vocation, but there are other shades and variations as well. There is celibacy that is a calling, freely chosen outside of religious life. And there is celibacy or periods of abstinence even within marriage. They all share an important trait: in saying no to one thing, you open your whole world to some other yes. The title of Luci Swindoll's book says it this way: *Wide My World, Narrow My Bed.*

Celibacy in the priesthood and religious life is embraced "for the sake of the kingdom of heaven." Those ordained as ministers of the church are "called to consecrate themselves with undivided heart to the Lord and to 'the affairs of the Lord'" (*Catechism,* 1579). It is, in part, this singleness of purpose, this single intention of the heart free from marital and familial distractions that makes the vocations of the priesthood and religious life so very powerful and efficacious.

The celibacy that I experience as a single person or that others who are married may experience out of necessity can also be offered up "for the sake of the kingdom," even though we may not experience that "undivided heart" in the same way that a person consecrated to religious life might. Celibacy in any shade can be a painful sacrifice, a state to be endured with patience and long-suffering, and we need bright reminders of the benefits of sexual abstinence.

When I am truly embracing the celibacy of my life— and I don't mean just physically—I am availing myself of a miraculous, satisfying world that's productive, fun, challenging, and deeply meaningful. When I get fixated on sex in and of itself—as opposed to sexuality and the joy I experience in being female—I start to feel frustrated, fearful, and inordinately entitled. Sex becomes "my right" rather than a gift given in love and self-sacrifice. Who needs that?

Waiting for sex until marriage seems an almost ludicrous proposition in our day, but I would ask you to consider this too: waiting for sexual expression until marriage is like buying fidelity insurance or working out at the gym. If we can wait for each other now, how much easier will it be to wait for each other during periods of separation in marriage, should they come? I think of soldiers separated from their spouses for months, even years at a time; a friend who was paralyzed in a car crash and will never be able to make love to his wife again; a friend suffering from a debilitating illness whose treatments leave her completely without libido. Sexy stuff, isn't it? But this is life! Will my friend's wife turn to him and say, "Well, honey, I'm sorry, but I have needs, so I'm going to sleep with another man"? Will the soldier returning from war say, "We were apart, it just got too difficult to be without sex, and so I found someone else"? If, as the reality and sacrifice of life unfold, we make our relationships more about sex than they truly are, we are setting ourselves up for, at best, superficiality or, at worst, soul-crushing disappointment.

Let's not join the world in making this a bigger issue than it is. I once heard a priest on retreat say that it is our job as Christians to discover ourselves as God the creator of all made us and then to be ourselves, and that to be your own person is the hardest thing of all. Celibacy and chastity are gifts that belong to very strong people, people unafraid of being their own person. I wish the world would stop looking at those who elect celibacy as sex-starved freaks or as people living "out of touch" with their sexuality or under some kind of puritan oppression. As if "free love" has brought us oceans of fulfillment! Have we noticed a significant improvement in quality of life as the result of spouse swapping, multiple-partner sex, or plain old promiscuity? Have those behaviors put us in better touch with ourselves and our sexuality?

Of course, celibacy is not easy, whether you live a religious, married, or single vocation. Our world is bombarded with sexual messages at every turn. Advertising drowns us in guarantees that just owning the right item—clothing, car, insurance, computer, whatever—will ensure us a satisfying sex life. Nearly every song on the radio centers on the theme of romantic love, as if no other kind of love is worth writing songs about. It's endless. It's difficult to keep a balanced perspective.

One of the most delicious gifts we've been given is just this: God created us male and female. What a magnificent idea! It makes life so very interesting. The church teaches that "physical, moral, and spiritual difference and complementarity are oriented toward the good of marriage and the flourishing of family life." The parameters that the church suggests for sexual expression are there not to suppress us, but to enliven us so that we might experience the gift of our sexuality in the fullest sense.

Sometimes I'm not the best steward of the gifts that God has given to me. As the church teaches, "Self-mastery is a long and exacting work," and "the effort required can be more intense in certain periods" (*Catechism,* 2342), like when I'm lonely, or soul-weary, or just feeling especially tempted and weak. In offering us these guidelines, the church wants to spare us the pain of soul corrosion that results from our falling. Fortunately, as with all sin, Jesus has paid the price for sexual immorality. This is good news.

I want to be a woman self-possessed, aware of my Creator, in love with the One I serve. When I encounter opportunities for sexual expression in a relationship, this is the question that presses my heart and mind: Whom do I serve? In the response of my heart, I hope to find the grace to enact an honest, dignified, loving, and purposeful choice.

（36）

THE PRO-LIFE LIFE

....

Before I formed you in the womb I knew you,
and before you were born I consecrated you.
—*Jeremiah 1:5*

IN HER NOBEL PEACE PRIZE acceptance speech in 1979, Mother Teresa said that the greatest destroyer of peace was abortion. She called it "a direct war," and in response to it, she and the Sisters of Charity, which she founded, issued a plea to any pregnant woman considering abortion: "Please don't destroy the child; we will take the child." The picture that accompanied the newspaper article about the speech is famous now. The diminutive figure of Mother Teresa, her head barely reaching above the podium, her body wrapped in the familiar blue-and-white sari, a microphone bent down like a limp tulip to reach her mouth. Looking at that picture and reading those words some years later, I distinctly remember thinking, *She is the most powerful woman on earth.*

What a mystery and a miracle, this gift of life. The psalmist rejoices in the work of our Creator this way: "My frame was not hidden from you, when I was being made in secret, intricately woven in the depths of the earth. Your eyes beheld my unformed substance. In your book were written all the days that were formed for me, when none of them as yet existed" (Psalm 139:15–16). The church teaches that life begins at conception and that all life is to be valued, no matter where it might fall on the line of development or decay—be it a three-day-old fetus or a bedridden ninety-three-year-old. We are all unique and unrepeatable. A person has value simply because she or he is a person. And in preaching a message of life, the church protects and upholds the right to life for all of us, from the strongest to the weakest, and I love her for it.

That's a high standard, and one I find difficult to follow at times. For example, one time when I was in need of a housemate, a friend offered to introduce me to a young Haitian woman who needed a place to stay. She was single, pregnant, and virtually alone in the world, and she had only been in the United States for a short time. At first, I was thrilled at the thought of taking her in. It was late fall, the season for "making room at the inn" for expectant mothers, so to speak. I thought about how exciting it would be, the anticipation of welcoming a new little person into the world hanging in the air of my house. I had helped a number of friends in the last months of their pregnancies and in delivery and found it enormously moving. And difficult.

Then I began to imagine a newborn crying in the middle of the night and a toddler destroying my stereo by putting pennies in the CD changer, and I thought, *Maybe this is more than I can handle? Maybe I'm not ready to open my home to this?* How quickly do I turn to my own interests.

I consulted a spiritual director, confessed my hypocrisy, and thought, *God, it's up to you. If she comes, she comes, and I will do my best to be welcoming and supportive and helpful.* Remember Mary at the Visitation, I told myself.

The Haitian woman didn't come. She found housing with a relative instead. I went back to looking for a housemate.

It was a good reminder for me that being pro-life, even at its most joyful, can also be inconvenient and messy and painful. It requires my most active, committed participation. *Life is costly and priceless.* Still, we try to measure it—by wealth, by health, by productivity, by accomplishments or the length of one's CV. Do I measure up? Do you? Who's to decide?

The church is clear:

> *Human life is sacred* because from its beginning it involves the creative action of God and it remains for ever in a special relationship with the Creator, who is its sole end. God alone is the Lord of life from its beginning until its end: no one can under any circumstance claim for himself the right directly to destroy an innocent human being (2258).

But it doesn't end there. The church also teaches that "love toward oneself remains a fundamental principle of morality. Therefore it is legitimate to insist on respect for one's own right to life. . . . Legitimate defense [of life] can be not only a right but a grave duty for one who is responsible for the lives of others" (*Catechism*, 2264–65).

For whose life are you responsible?

Out of love for myself, out of respect for my own life and all the privileges and rights inherent in it, I must defend those who cannot defend themselves. I do not get to pick and choose when and where people might need help along the way of life, whether the person is a three-day-old fetus without a voice, a bedridden ninety-three-year-old who no longer recognizes his own children, or a poor soul in purgatory. As a Catholic, I must walk out this pro-life life, putting my money, my time, and my prayers where my mouth is.

I want to live as Mother Teresa, that most powerful woman, lived, welcoming life in sickness and in health, in convenience and in sacrifice, in glorious beauty and in gruesome defect. Of course, "pro-life" issues are not limited to abortion. They also include embryonic stem cell research, sex selection of our children, euthanasia, the Pill, natural family planning, capital punishment, and so on. The church stands unabashedly, with all her members, even as disparate as our opinions may be, in the thick of it all. Personally, I want the kind of devotion and clarity of heart that called Mother Teresa to live so aggressively, so baldly in support of the sanctity of life, no matter the cost to her. I find that I can best do so within the arms of my beloved church. From this view, I accept and believe with all my heart the church's teaching. Always on the periphery of my view is this knowledge: when Mary went to visit Elizabeth, John leaped in Elizabeth's womb at the sound of Mary's greeting (Luke 1:41, 44).

And there are more big questions ahead of us. Are we discovering evidence of the long-term physical harm that abortion causes women? Will genetic engineering change the nature of the relationship between parent and child into consumer and product? Is embryonic stem cell research really necessary in light of the advances adult stem cell research seems capable of producing? These are big questions, and they need to be embraced and pondered by all of us. We cannot leave them solely for others—politicians in Washington or scientists in laboratories—to decide.

There were years when I adopted a pro-choice platform, but I confess it was not out of reason or a belief that a pro-choice stance was true, but more out of fear of confronting the difficult choices and sacrifices that being pro-life meant. I had to become willing to give up the comfortable righteousness I'd worked up for myself and accept that I wasn't being truthful, and that following what I knew to be truthful would require more of me than I'd ever been willing to give before. The expression *pro-choice* seems ridiculous to me now, because I understand that to choose abortion or euthanasia or to destroy embryos in the name of research is really to choose death. I have a deeper understanding of and respect for those who, with careful thought and reasoned application, use the phrase *culture of death*. I hate that phrase, but I understand what it means.

These are hard words, I know. They will make some people very angry. I used to be one of them. Whatever emotions these words may stir up, we can take those feelings and thoughts and questions straight to Jesus. I am convinced that he will greet the earnest heart, however uncertain or angry or weak, just as he greeted Jeremiah: "Child, I knew you before you were formed, and I have consecrated you to live. I have given you this gift. Let me show you truth so that you may love it and live freely."

This is possibly the most heartbreaking issue the church faces, but Jesus will help us find our way. And at his feet, I believe we will always find life waiting to embrace us, arms alive and welcoming and warm for all.

37

The Promise of the Holy Spirit

A new heart I will give you, and a new spirit
I will put within you; and I will remove from
your body the heart of stone and give you a
heart of flesh.
—Ezekiel 36:26

THIS IS THE IMAGE THAT comes to my mind: I am frozen in ice. Not your average ice, but thick, dark, glacial ice. Something from the Ice Age, so deep and so heavy that you can barely make out that there is a person—me—trapped deep within it. Then the Father appears and begins considering this big lump of ice   kind of surveying it, moving around it in circles and pondering it from every angle, not looking the least bit concerned, only knowing. Then Jesus joins him and immediately reaches out to touch the ice. And when he does, it melts away under his fingers. The two discuss the situation a bit, considering the best options for my removal from this dark and lifeless place. They do so very calmly, almost matter-of-fact; there is the distinct absence of doubt that I will be saved. Then the Holy Spirit comes in, and slowly, simply with his presence, turns up the heat. It is clear that the goal is not to fry me or burn me, but to free me. Slowly, drop by drop, the ice melts away, sometimes in torrents and other times with slow constancy; and the three of them, Father, Son, and Holy Spirit, stand there patiently, just watching, waiting, ready to catch me should I suddenly fall out. In the end, it is the strong, warm hands of Jesus that reach in and gently excise me, free me completely from this icy death.

Then he holds me tightly, almost ferociously, and long, even after I have stopped weeping.

To fall in love with Jesus, to become his follower, is to be given a new heart. One of the chief surgeons in this operation is the Holy Spirit. Jesus promised us that he would leave us the "Advocate," "the Spirit of truth," "the Holy Spirit, whom the Father will send in my name," and that the Advocate would remain with us forever (John 14:16–17, 26). Jesus told Judas, "Those who love me will keep my word, and my Father will love them, and we will come to them and make our home with them" (John 14:23). It is the Holy Spirit that delivers Father and Son to our door. Believe me, when Jesus makes himself at home in you through the Holy Spirit, it is impossible to stay frozen—in immaturity, fear, shame, faithlessness, resentment, greed, entitlement, spite, depression, self-pity, or selfishness. You become softened and made real through the warm and gentle touch of the Master. You become home to Love. It's a promise.

Now there are those conversions that the Holy Spirit brings on like a lightning bolt, immediate and dramatic, striking the Sauls of the world to the ground. At Pentecost, tongues of fire descended upon the apostles to give them the ability to speak in many languages about the powerful deeds of God. There, the Holy Spirit was fire and heat and passion and power.

Often when I sit down to write or to pray, I light a candle. Sometimes it is a reminder of that burning passion of the Holy Spirit, and it is also a petition—in lighting the candle, I ask the Holy Spirit to give me the ability to speak of God's powerful deeds in my own life. At other times, the prayer is that the Holy Spirit will burn away any obstacle keeping me from being close to him and from knowing him. But more often than not, it is a petition for warmth of heart and for the gentle light of guidance, protection, and inspiration in a world that too often has grown dark.

The nice thing about lightning bolts is that they come and go quickly. For those of us whose conversion is more like the thawing out of a block of ice, it can feel protracted and mighty painful.

For me, the Holy Spirit, the Advocate, has been like my personal heart softener, softening me not to the point of passing out and becoming a doormat, but so that I can finally relax into my humanity, into the arms of Jesus, and accept his grace and goodness and love. It seems counter-intuitive, but we need to relax and let the Holy Spirit do the work rather than try harder, push more, withstand, strive, and cling.

This is another way to think about it: if I am riding my bike up a steep hill, I have to become soft, relaxed. I still have to be engaged with the hill and the work of riding a bike, but if I don't soften, one of two things will likely happen: I'll stall out on the bike and fall over, or I'll injure myself. The same is true in my faith life: if I try to adhere rigidly to all the rules and regulations and forget about the heart, I'm going to injure myself or others, or I'm going to stall out and stop growing closer to Jesus. He left me the Advocate to make sure that doesn't happen.

So many gifts the Spirit bestows on those who lean into him to receive a flesh-and-blood heart. Consider the gifts of his presence: the well-known passage from St. Paul's letter to the Galatians lists the fruit of the Spirit as "love, joy, peace, patience, kindness, generosity, faithfulness, gentleness, and self-control" (5:22–23). This isn't a spiritual shopping list but the promise of God. This is the new spirit that the prophet Ezekiel promised, arriving one gorgeous virtue at a time.

Bring your flames, your tongues of fire, Holy Spirit, to give me the ability to live in Truth and melt away anything keeping me from being close to Jesus.

38

THE NAMES OF GOD

···

Adonai, hallowed be Thy name.
—*Jesus Christ*

GOD'S NAME IS SO POWERFUL that he devoted a whole commandment to its care and attention. God identified himself to Moses on Mount Sinai using names Moses would know and respect: "'The LORD, the God of your ancestors, the God of Abraham, the God of Isaac, and the God of Jacob': . . . This is my name forever, and this my title for all generations" (Exodus 3:15). Later, the Jewish people came to believe that the name of God was so holy that they dared not even speak it. Zechariah declared that "on that day the LORD will be one and his name one" (14:9). When Jesus was teaching his disciples how to pray, he dedicated an entire clause right at the top to honoring God's name. When Jesus came forward and announced himself to the soldiers who had come to arrest him in the Garden of Gethsemane, they fell to the ground, just at the sound of "I am he."

I AM WHO I AM.

In naming, we identify; we come to know. In naming, we draw closer, grow more intimate. In naming, we love. We come to know ourselves and we begin to experience relationship. In sharing our name with another, we open the door to communion. Our name is the first door to our heart.

Names carry enormous weight. I have known for as long as I can remember that my name, Elizabeth Michaela, means "God's oath" and "warrior." I have been affected and inspired by this knowledge, hoping that I can live up to my name's significance, "God's devoted warrior"; I love the idea that I am suited, even in my name, for spiritual battle. Later, when I chose Virginia as my confirmation name because it was the name of my sister and derived from the Blessed Virgin Mary, I garnered even more "heavenly juice" and, in my view, feminine strength.

In her wonderful work *Walking on Water: Reflections on Faith and Art,* Madeleine L'Engle writes, "We live in a world that would reduce us to our social security numbers." We label a box "2001 tax receipts" and throw our tax returns in it—you'll find no receipts from any other year in there, no toasters or socks. We have the silverware drawer and the health and beauty aisle. We label our leaders, our artists, our children. And these labels contain, quantify, limit, and take all of the guesswork out of it. You simply look at a label, and you have to go no further; you don't have to open the sock drawer or the ketchup bottle to know what's inside. I doubt that if you showed up at the White House and said, "A Republican has sent me; let me inside!"

the gates would open up to you. If, on the other hand, you had a name to drop—George Washington, Abraham Lincoln, Martin Luther King Jr., Mother Teresa—then you might see some action. Names are more powerful than labels because they imply relationship.

A name does little to contain or control. A name invites; it opens; it lets others in to discover the mysterious, fearsome, and limitless territories inside. You might want to live with the certainty of a label, and your life may be free from certain fears because of it, but I wonder if it might be free of love as well.

L'Engle writes, "To be given a name is an act of intimacy as powerful as any act of love. . . . To name is to love. To be Named is to be loved. So in a very true sense the great [artistic] works which help us to be more named also love us and help us to love." Heaven has named you and me, just as surely as heaven has named Jesus, and that gloriously merciful and tender act is helping us love, love, love.

Messiah.

The great challenge in contemplating the names of God is to avoid the convenience and security of labeling, for in labeling, we murder off life itself, and all the creativity, possibilities, miracles, healing, and hope that accompanies it.

L'Engle speaks of the difficulty in teaching young writers who want to write "Christian fiction" and are very much concerned with this label; they want to know what, exactly, it means to be a "Christian writer." In trying to assemble characteristics that would make their writing "Christian," these young writers become distracted and are unable to really understand the task at hand. "Their chief job," she writes, "is to learn the techniques of fiction, to read as many of the great writers as possible, and to learn from them, without worrying about how often they went to church, or to what denomination they belonged. The important thing to look for is whether or not they could write."

The same is true when I am endeavoring to understand this "Catholic" life. The important thing for me in looking to the name of Jesus is not to get caught up in the convenient labels that the Pharisees wanted to contain him with. My job is to learn as much about him as I can, to read his word and wonder whether or not he could love.

As I grow older, it takes less to draw me into contemplation. A favorite meditation is to simply list as many of the names of God as I can think of and quietly sit with them, allowing them to keep me company: Lord of Heaven and Earth. King of the Jews. Jesus. Son of Man. Teacher. Prince of Peace. Emmanuel. Comforter. Healer. Mighty One. Creator. Abba. Father. Holy One. Beautiful One. Beloved. Just try putting God in a box with a label on it. Who would want a god like that, a god you could pull off the shelf dusty and musty at your whim? Where is the power in that?

Jesus' love was so fearsome and expansive that he didn't just hang out with "prostitutes and tax collectors." No, he kept company with Mary Magdalene and Zacchaeus.

Scripture assures us that just as God knows all the stars he appointed, he knows all of us by name: "Who is my equal? says the Holy One. Lift up your eyes on high and see: Who created these? He who brings out their host and numbers them, calling them all by name; because he is great in strength, mighty in power, not one is missing" (Isaiah 40:25–26). It is calling on his name, Jesus, when "two or three are gathered" that invites his presence. Not our goodness, not our rightness, not our labels and thoughts and fears. His name.

When I am sitting with his names, sitting in the company of my Jesus, he is not just sitting in the company of some sinner. He's sitting with me: *Elizabeth Michaela Virginia.*

When we can love like that, our world gets expansive, limitless, not boxed and predictable. It is in his naming us that we are found; it is in our naming him that we are saved and loved without limit.

39

God Comes to Meet Us

*My seeing ripens things, and they come
toward me to meet and be met.*
—Rainer Maria Rilke

THE SENTENCE *God comes to meet us* says a great deal about the nature of our relationship with Jesus. It is the title of chapter 2 of the *Catechism* and sums up beautifully my experience with God. *He comes to me.* I do nothing to earn his friendship. As the *Catechism* says, "Through an utterly free decision, God has revealed himself and given himself to man. This he does by revealing the mystery, his plan of loving goodness, formed from all eternity in Christ, for the benefit of all men. God has fully revealed this plan by sending us his beloved Son, our Lord Jesus Christ, and the Holy Spirit" (50). Revealed, loving, eternal, beneficial. It is a precious and tender gift, essential to my faith and my life, to accept the truth behind each of these words and to pay attention as they bear themselves out in my life.

Revealed

First we need to recognize what has been revealed. Christ is the fulfillment of the revelation. God reveals himself to us through Jesus, his Son, in order that we might come to know him and love him and share in his divine nature as his sons and daughters. The church teaches that God reveals himself to people gradually through sacred Scripture, which he authored, and living sacred Tradition, which the church upholds. We also believe that Scripture is complete. "God has said everything in his Word. . . . There will be no further revelation" (*Catechism,* 65). That's big picture Revelation—with a capital *R.*

I find comfort in these words, however, even when I need "day-to-day" revelation. In meditating upon "God comes to meet me," I can trust that even if I don't know the answer to my questions now, at some point, all things will be revealed. Sometimes, I just need to sit with the question and wait for God. I can trust that I will not be left to my own devices. God's "plan of loving goodness" has been revealed. This revelation is ongoing in the big picture and ongoing in my day-to-day picture too. When I'm feeling confused, I can go to Jesus, to the Gospels, to Scripture and tap into the grace and comfort of revelation. It also helps put day-to-day experiences in perspective by focusing on big picture revelation. No matter what's going on today, in the end, love wins.

Loving

Think of the most loving thing you could do for another, perhaps your own child. What would it be? To provide food, clothing, shelter? A college education and ballet lessons? An embrace when they are hurting most of all? A life of sacrifice? Discipline and correction? This word *loving* is an important one to keep in mind because sometimes the plan doesn't always feel so loving. Feelings are important, and I believe that God does care about our feelings, but I don't bow down and worship my feelings either. They pass, they shift, they swell and diminish. And they can be painful. Job, the icon of Old Testament suffering, is reminded that God "wounds, but he binds up; he strikes, but his hand heals" (Job 5:18). It's like a heart transplant; having a surgeon cut through my chest is not the most appealing, painless procedure, but it just might save my life. Sometimes, God's plan involves "transplants" of numerous varieties. They hurt sometimes. I do well to remember that God's plan is loving, even in the painful spots.

Eternal

There's one plan, one revelation, one Savior who exists through all eternity. I can trust that the loving portion of the plan of revelation does not run out, that this is love for the long haul. It is good for me to consider this word *eternal* and apply it to my day. When I am walking through the world, certainly present to the moment but recognizing it as a part of the eternal continuum, it helps to keep traffic jams, illnesses, high rents and low salaries, even loneliness in perspective. Am I living for the day or living for heaven? Or, better yet, am I living *this day for the long haul*?

Beneficial

Nothing happens in the plan that God cannot turn to my benefit. Nothing. Nothing is out of the purview of my Father. The problems of evil and suffering are too broad to examine here, but I will say from my own experience that nothing of my life has gone to waste. It is a mystery of grace and redemption that Jesus can take my sin and suffering and turn them into spiritual gold. It is a mystery of mercy that Jesus can observe my arrogance, remove it, and replace it with confidence; it is a miracle that he can observe my fear of what others think of me, remove it, and replace it with peace and confidence in him.

There is a final word to add when considering the revealed, loving, eternal, beneficial plan of God as he comes to meet me: *free*. I don't earn this plan of salvation. I can't buy it. I can't manipulate it out of God. I can't argue my way into heaven or work my way in there. God chooses to come to me. Freely God gives himself to me. Freely he sends his Son. Freely he sends the Holy Spirit. Freely he comes to meet me.

40

VISIT THE IMPRISONED:
A CORPORAL WORK OF MERCY

Love your neighbor as yourself.
—Matthew 22:39

MOTHER TERESA ONCE SAID THAT if you knew everyone's story, you'd love everyone. The story I came to know was Tammy's (not her real name). When we met, Tammy had yet to reach her twenty-fifth birthday. It was her second stint in prison, this time on a charge of armed robbery. At home, she had two young children, whom Tammy's father was raising. She rarely saw them. To say that there was sadness in her eyes is an understatement. They were overtaken by a profound vacancy and despair. I have yet to see a look like that in another human being.

Before coming to visit Tammy, I had been inside a prison only once, to interview a prison guard for a piece I was writing for the *Anchorage Daily News*. He took me on a tour around the facility, including a high-security area. Men in this section were held in their cells twenty-three hours a day; the twenty-fourth hour they spent walking and exercising in a small paved courtyard area or a community room with a few tables and chairs. When I entered, they immediately stood in their cells, hovering behind Plexiglas like aged and tired "doggies in the window," hungry for attention. Each came to the door of his cell; some pressed themselves against the glass. "They don't see women that often," the guard said.

These are not human beings, not men, I thought. How does someone end up in a place like this, with only an hour each day for venturing outside a room no larger than a fitting room at Nordstrom?

Years later, I would learn how from Tammy.

The program for which I volunteered required that you meet with a prisoner once a week for several months to discuss "decision-making skills." The prisoners were given homework and short reading assignments about how to make good decisions and how to recognize in advance the consequences of bad decisions. It was basically a visiting program, meant to give prisoners a break from their usual routine. We who visited them, as much as we meant well, were like a "reward" for good behavior.

On my first visit with Tammy, she told me, "I didn't do it." She said that she had been asleep in the backseat of her boyfriend's car when he and a friend decided to hold up a 7-Eleven. Tammy barely knew her own mother, for she had been imprisoned by the time Tammy was fifteen and was still in prison. I didn't ask her what her mother had been charged with, and Tammy did not offer an explanation.

Our visits reminded me at times of a scene out of a Flannery O'Connor novel, dark and humorous for their pretense filled with characters desperately hoping for a different reality. Tammy—wildly emotional, over-enthusiastic, cheerful one minute and brooding the next, wishing so to be the wrongfully accused devoted mother of two, fighting against the lions of injustice from a prison cell. And me—wishing so that I had the words, the skills, the maturity, the depth and desire of a Mother Teresa to bring life and light into the heart of a dark and wounded soul. And realizing with flat clarity how far short I fell, how widely I missed the mark, like a basketball dimpled for lack of air hitting the hard gym floor and rolling absolutely nowhere.

One of the reasons I love being Catholic is for the unflinching character it asks of you. I think of so many members of the church's fold who have lived out Christ's command to love one another despite the ugly realities that might accompany such a mission—angels and warriors of social justice such as Mother Teresa, Dorothy Day, St. Francis of Assisi, Bd. Pier Giorgio Frasatti. It is easy to love my perfect and smiling and healthy newborn nephew, for example. It is much more difficult for me to pour myself out for Tammy. "Love your neighbor as yourself" seems an impossibly difficult charge, but I love the fact that Jesus sets the bar so high, and so low, and so wide, and so real. It was a charge he would live out and die for. He walked among the lepers and tax collectors and poor and prostitutes. He poured himself out for all, even unto death on a cross, with murderers hanging by his side. Because of this, I can rise again and again. Because of him, I can be transformed, saved, loved into eternity. So can Tammy.

I wish I could say that my corporal work of mercy in visiting Tammy and in attempting to befriend her and help her yielded great fruit. That somehow we became close friends, or that her life was somehow miraculously reformed. The truth is that I don't know what became of her. We were not encouraged to exchange personal information; in fact, we were forbidden from doing so. The truth is that I didn't feel comfortable staying in contact with her. The truth is that I was relieved when my appointed visits were complete. And I was sad, believing that I had failed Tammy.

I realize that not everyone has the same vocation. There are angels of mercy who visit with the imprisoned, and their hearts are filled with joy to overflowing. I have sung for Jazz Fighting Hunger concerts and led the rosary at a local assisted living facility and found those works far better suited to my skills, experience, and temperament. The list of corporal works is not terribly long, but there is room for finding one's niche in them; we are directed, implored by Jesus and the church to *feed the hungry, give drink to the thirsty, clothe the naked, shelter the homeless, visit the sick, bury the dead,* and *visit the imprisoned.* Maybe we donate money or time or talent or other resources.

There are many aspects to fulfilling the command to love one another, and it is prudent to bear in mind this notion from missionary James Hudson Taylor: before God sends a person off to Africa, he puts tenderness for Africa in that person's heart. I am aware of the necessity and wisdom of praying for direction in my vocation, especially when it comes to works of mercy. I am reminded that in loving my neighbor as myself, I must first *be myself* and use the gifts that God has given me.

But I will never forget Tammy, or the myriad men and women sitting in prisons even now. Recently, I met a married couple who run a prison ministry, and I was delighted to learn that they distribute my first book on the rosary to prisoners. They said that the prisoners "gobble them up," and I am so very, very grateful and humbled to perhaps have found a way, by no strength of my own, through no grace or virtue of my own, to at last visit the imprisoned in a meaningful way. If that's not a definition of mercy, I don't know what is.

41

BELONGING TO THE UNIVERSAL CHURCH

The order and harmony of the created world
results from the diversity of beings and from
the relationships which exists among them
—Catechism, 341

Two of my friends have a house in Maine, which they generously offered to share with me and my writing buddy Lil one long fall weekend. So, listening to the Red Sox game on the radio and sharing a whoop when they won, we trekked up to South Bristol together to hang out in their house and go "leaf peeping," jog along the Maine coastline, eat the best blueberry pancakes in the world served on paper plates at the local diner, sleep in, and feast on the hostess's gourmet cooking—spinach dumplings and fresh apple cobbler. Everything a weekend in Maine is meant for.

My friends had discovered that the oldest church in New England, St. Patrick's, was not too far down the road, and so we all piled in the car on Sunday morning and headed for Mass. Because the church building is quite small, and because the trees are so breathtaking, Mass was held in a wooded area next to the church, underneath a perfect canopy of fall foliage. Occasionally leaves would drop during Mass to rest on our heads and laps. A family with four young girls sitting in front of us spent most of the service occupied with a small insect that one of the girls had trapped gently in her cupped hands. Lil and I spotted a few Yankees hats in the crowd and, being from Boston and just days away from defeating the Yankees for the pennant, tried our best to offer them the sign of peace when it came time. We sang songs—rather poorly, as Catholics sometimes do—and we listened to the readings, on park benches instead of pews, outside in the chilly fall air.

Before Father began his sermon, he asked if there were any visitors in the congregation. Hands flew up around us. St. Patrick's is the kind of historical site that naturally attracts visitors and tourists. He asked that visitors to the parish call out where we were from so he could welcome us all, and hence the litany began: Boston, Toronto, Minneapolis, North Carolina, New Brunswick, California, Florida, Germany. It went on for some time, including many states and several continents. Father was careful to include everyone. We were young and old and educated and not and healthy and ill and every shade of life in between. We all joined in the same Mass, shared the same sign of peace, took the same holy Host. The same scarlet and orange leaves fell on us when we bowed our heads and asked for God's blessing.

When Holy Communion was finished and Mass was nearly over, there were a few announcements. One woman stood up and asked for prayers for her husband sick with cancer. "Because I believe in the power of prayer," she said, "we'll be here at the front and would ask for your prayers for my husband's healing after the Mass." I was deeply moved as I watched a small crowd assemble to pray over the man as soon as the service ended.

The rest of us left as we came, loud and laughing, babies crying and older folks moving slowly, taking their time. Messy, happy, hurting, wonderful humanity dispersing to our far corners. The universal church.

Catholic means universal, all-inclusive, or whole. It means there's room for everybody and everyone is invited. We are the "assembly of those whom God's Word . . . gathers together to form the People of God, and who themselves, nourished with the Body of Christ, become the Body of Christ" (*Catechism,* 777). The church teaches that all humankind belongs to the church. "By her very mission, 'the Church . . . travels the same journey as all humanity and shares the same earthly lot with the world'" (*Catechism,* 854).

The church exists to serve and unite the whole human race, to share the same lot. I like that idea, even though I don't do as good a job of remembering and practicing it as I'd like. It is always a good reminder to ponder the word *universal.*

The desire to belong is a natural human inclination. Sometimes the challenge is to leave room for others, to occupy the space that we have been given—no more, no less. Belonging also implies ownership and responsibility, and these aspects sometimes ruffle our spiritual feathers. We like to belong, to be a part of something, but when that belonging requires responsibility—such as going to the front of the church to pray for a sick brother—when it ties us to other human beings who are far from perfect, who step on our toes or steal our toast at the breakfast table or our promotions at work, that's when things can get a little uncomfortable. I love that we have the Mystical Body as a means to surrender to this lesson over and over again, until our final refinement in heaven. I don't know about you, but I *need* it.

A friend called me this morning to confess a dramatic bout of self-pity and self-centeredness. We laughed together as we confirmed that yes, everyone was out to get her; yes, she was suffering more than any other person on the planet had ever suffered before; and yes, it was likely that God had completely forgotten her and only her while remembering to bless all his other children with lives of bliss and ease. Sometimes expressing such thoughts aloud to another is the best way to purge them. In fact, my friend was fundamentally well and had much for which she was grateful. Part of the miracle and beauty of belonging to the universal church is just this: if one member suffers, we all suffer, and if one member is honored, we all rejoice. We exist in service to and support of one another. We're not in this great journey only for our personal sanctification.

And it gets even better. The church teaches that we have all been given gifts, or charisms, to help build one another up, and that while we are "one body," there is also great diversity among our members and the gifts that we have been given. This is the fun part! Not only is there room for every gift, but there is a specific need for it.

We bring these charisms to the universal church—both visible and invisible—to experience union as one body, with all the sacrifices, aches, pains, and pleasures that come with it. These charisms help keep us from two extremes: either placing ourselves on a pedestal, thinking we need no one, or burying ourselves in the opinions of others, never standing on the feet God has given us.

It is cause for wonder that in some mystical way our Father both needs us to be who we were created to be and yet allows us to choose to be who we want to be. As María Ruiz Scaperlanda writes so beautifully:

> God needs us to live out who we are in the world.
> He needs me to be me, fully me, truly me—for
> my family, my neighbors, my work mates, my
> parish community, my city, my state. There are no
> coincidences . . . this pilgrimage is not random or
> generic or communal, but personal and specific. I

was birthed into this moment by a Creator whose vision for the world not only includes but requires me. I am an explicit part of his plan!

I am an explicit part of the plan, but I am not God. I cannot save people. I cannot change them or the world. Only heaven can do that. If I cooperate and allow myself—my whole self, all my gifts and charisms—to belong to the church, to be in the service of the church, then I can be an instrument in that orchestra of change and salvation. But the breath to make the instrument resonate must come from Jesus, from the Holy Spirit. It is not something that I can manufacture on my own.

Universality addresses our human loneliness, but it is much more than that. It is what leads us to our purpose as well. When we offer our gifts, our very lives to the service of others, we are living what the church teaches to be the highest vocation. In Jesus, "there is no longer Jew or Greek, there is no longer slave or free, there is no longer male and female; for all of you are one. . . . And if you belong to Christ, then you are Abraham's offspring, heirs according to the promise" (Galatians 3:28–29).

It is God's heart to unify all his children, to bring us all into his family. That is the mission of the church, to extend the love of Jesus to the entire human race. All our diverse personalities, gifts, and charisms are meant to help in that effort. "All nations form but one community. . . .

[A]ll share a common destiny, namely God. His providence, evident goodness, and saving designs extend to all" (*Catechism*, 842).

Even to Yankees fans.

For "Rim," who lovingly indoctrinated me in the canon of baseball.

PART FIVE

Rhythms of the Faith

42

DAILY MASS

....

THE CHURCH WHERE I ATTEND daily Mass, in Harvard Square, boasts the Boston Boy Choir and St. Paul Men's Schola. They give the phrase "shake the rafters" a whole new meaning. Their grand processionals and swelling choruses during Sunday Mass are immense and filling and delicate. On more than one occasion, I've been brought to tears at those penetrating voices, like angels coming to visit. Such music must make heaven smile.

But at daily Mass, we rarely sing, the ten or twenty of us who rush in on our lunch hour to get quiet and still and to pay a visit before rushing back out to the rest of our day. The sermons are usually short and to the point, almost perfunctory. The sign of peace is usually a quick nod or wave in the general direction of another. There are no processions, no musical gymnastics, no ballyhoo of any kind. Mass, quick and simple.

It is perhaps ironic that I, a musician and performer, prefer daily Mass. But the older I get, the greater appreciation

I have for keeping things simple. And that is part of the appeal of daily Mass. Those in attendance really want to be there; we feel drawn there because once on the weekends is simply not enough. No matter what's happening at work, no matter what's on my mind, Mass always makes things better. My circumstances and problems may not change at all; in fact, they may get more challenging or decline further still. But the life of faith is not about changing life; it's about changing me. Attending Mass does change me, grace me, and enable me to attend to whatever circumstances meet me when I walk out the church doors into the waiting world.

I don't go to daily Mass because I'm so devout, or because I feel obligated, or because I want to look pious (as if I could!). I go to daily Mass because my sweet Jesus is there, awaiting my company, looking forward to my arrival, welcoming and ready to whisper to my spirit, "My daughter, I hear you. My daughter, I love you; come and sit with me awhile." How can I resist his gentle invitation? Who can resist the insistent invitation of their beloved? I go to daily Mass because my God isn't a Sundays-only kind of God. I go to daily Mass because I need God daily, and I need a daily kind of God.

It is a tremendous grace and a precious luxury that we have the option to attend Mass every day. Do I think God deserves the Sunday majesty and magnificence of the Boston Boy Choir and their processionals? Of course, God deserves all of that—our very best, most loving, most effusive adoration. But as I move through this life of faith, I find that I need a God who whispers more often than he roars. A God who whispers because my heart is so quiet and still before him, so free of distractions, that he no longer has to shout. A God who whispers because we have grown so close that we can take intimate delight in sharing things meant only for each other. I need a God who is that much in love with me, who is that devoted to me daily. This is Jesus, my Beloved. How can I help but respond with daily devotion to him?

43

THE FEAST OF THE EPIPHANY

....

IT STARTED WITH A PROPHET'S vision. Generations later it was resumed in a rising star and the dreams of kings. It continued with an escape along an unplanned road. It continues still in each of us on the journey. Christ's manifestation to the world is celebrated in the Feast of the Epiphany. Epiphany is the "public" announcement that Emmanuel has come, and now, at long last, *God is with us.* As a child, I thought of this feast as the tired denouement of the excitement of Christmas, but as I grow older, I am becoming fonder of how the Christmas season builds to this miraculous adventure and then invites us all to join along. But there are many distractions to pull me off course. It is easy for Christmas—its meaning and its message—to become obscured.

The commercial distractions and cultural expectations are cause enough for depression. The pressures to have fun, shop 'til you drop, and enjoy time with family and friends can be daunting and unnatural. Maybe our bank accounts are stretched and presents are scarce; maybe our families and friends are far away or far from the perfect picture of intimacy and health. Maybe instead of serene and satisfied we feel lonely and lost. It is possible that we have forgotten our way to Bethlehem and innocence.

I think God gave us the Feast of the Epiphany to remind us that even the wise men needed guidance, a light to follow, a heavenly body to show them the way. Not only were they given guidance, but they were also given safe passage through a thrilling adventure: the search for salvation, for the truth. We are all invited to join them on the journey. And it's no different for us than it was for the wise men: we are given plenty of help to find Christ's manifestation in our lives. These days, it's not just the stars that lead us to Bethlehem.

My favorite Christmas card this year came from a writer friend, one of my favorite "stars." Her card was delivered a week or so "late" (ironically, closer to Epiphany), and the red-ink inscription in the far upper left-hand corner inside read simply, "Rejoice, girl." I love the way she can boil down all the ado to the smallest and most significant common denominator while giving little thought to whether she's doing things picture-perfectly. She is what I call "her own unit." She is driven by her love for Jesus, is unafraid of the consequences of that love, and experiences a profound willingness to be exactly the creature God created her to be. The crystal simplicity and depth of her faith, especially as it pours forth in her writing, always draws me closer to heaven.

There have been countless stars whom I did not know personally, writers and painters and musicians whose work, whether they recognized it or not, was divinely inspired and revealed to me new visions about God and God's world, giving me new mysteries to ponder. If I ask for eyes to see them, my life is filled with stars guiding me to heaven at every moment. There are stars that allow me to see great distances ahead, and stars that allow me to see only what's immediately in front of me, but they all help me see my way to Jesus.

We all have our guiding lights that lead us to Jesus, people and passions and places that help us find our way, grow closer to Jesus, and find God's presence. If you don't think you have any, or if you feel that your life is particularly dim at the moment, ask God to fill your life with stars, and watch what happens.

The passage from the Old Testament that is read at the Feast of the Epiphany comes from the prophet Isaiah. It reads, "Rise up in splendor, Jerusalem! Your light has come, the glory of the Lord shines upon *you*" (see Isaiah 60:1). In other words, *Rejoice, girl.*

Have you forgotten your way to Bethlehem? Would you like to go back? Don't worry, God's light is shining upon you, and he is eager to fill the heavens of your life with stars to light and guide—and to help you become a rising star for others. In that, there is great, luminous cause to rejoice.

44

Ash Wednesday

Were you so inclined, you could hide the fact that you are Catholic on almost any day of the year, but on Ash Wednesday, you blow any cover you might have had. On this holy day, which begins the season of Lent, we receive ashes in the sign of the cross on our foreheads with this prayer: "Remember that you are dust, and unto dust you shall return." Call me nuts, but I've always found relief in that prayer. Something about the smallness of me, the smallness of this life set against the reality of eternity brings comfort and perspective and hope.

When I was a kid, Lent meant fish sticks and tartar sauce in the lunchroom on Fridays and grilled cheese sandwiches for dinner. It meant little Rice Bowl collection cups that we filled with our pennies and spare change, and trying to give up something that we really liked a lot—candy, television, popcorn. I don't know when I came to the understanding of self-mortification, of what it meant to deny oneself on purpose, for a purpose, for penance and as a means of purification. But the ashes on our foreheads were the visible reminders that we needed this period of self-mortification, and that Ash Wednesday was our official entry into this season.

Last Ash Wednesday, along with a swarm of people around the country, I went to see Mel Gibson's blockbuster movie *The Passion of the Christ*. There we were, the forty or so of us from the young-adult group at the Harvard Catholic Student Center, standing in line for the 7 PM showing in downtown Boston, ashes crossed on our foreheads. I noted curiously a heightened sense of belonging as we waited together. We were all dust, we were all in it together, we all shared the same profound need for Jesus, and we wore that need on our very foreheads—a kind of spiritual tattoo.

On the Ash Wednesdays of my teenage years, I felt extremely self-conscious about my ashen cross as I moved through crowds of non-Catholics at the bus stop or in the library. Of course, children that age often poke fun at such things; certainly, a little self-consciousness is to be expected when you're thirteen or fourteen. But every year, I still feel just a tinge of self-consciousness as I walk out of Mass on Ash Wednesday. Not so much because I'm worried what non-Catholics walking down the street might think of me, but because I wish for an opportunity to explain the importance of the tradition and offer an invitation to embrace it. I wish that in that ashen cross on my forehead they could see what is in my heart, the gratitude and humility I feel on that day as on no other. I wish they could read in that black cross, "I'm not dirty; I'm grateful." There's just so much hope in that little black smudge.

Harvard is an especially diverse place, which is one of its greatest strengths, in my opinion. Walking through Harvard Square on Ash Wednesday after Mass, it was a satisfying thing to observe the many shades and sizes that "Catholic" comes in by noting the people with ashen smudges walking to and fro. They were young, old, black, white, scientist, poet, garbageman, pizza delivery driver, student, professor, doctor, athlete, office manager, executive, police officer, artist, parent. It was an endless list, and that is pretty much the point of Catholicism and one of my favorite things about it. We celebrate the fact that there is a place for everyone. We all have the same need. We are made of the same flesh and blood, and in the end, we're all dust and ashes. Andrew Greeley put it this way: "Catholics cluster, they bond, they converge, they swarm. . . . We draw our boundaries out as wide as we can and, in our better moments, include within the boundaries even those who think they are outside." I like this image of clustering, swarming Catholics just out of Ash Wednesday Mass. What better occasion to cluster and swarm and take comfort and strength in our common experience?

Like so many aspects of faith and believing, it is a paradox I can point to and a mystery I cannot fully know: I am dust, and at the same time I am the apple of my Father's eye. I am known by my Creator and set to a life of blessing and favor. He loves me enough to save me, to raise me from the dust of this earth and one day bring me to heaven to live with him for eternity.

Ash Wednesday is our reminder to celebrate the mysterious mercy of a God who would love us this much. Ash Wednesday is an opportunity to raise our thoughts to the almighty One and ask for mercy that we cannot earn. On Ash Wednesday we can trust that the answer of heaven to those who ask for mercy in earnest will always be "There is plenty for everyone, no matter your shade, your educational background, the size of your bank account, or the depth and breadth of your sin. Heaven never runs out of mercy. Jesus has paid the price for all forever."

On Ash Wednesday, a vivid picture sometimes comes to my mind. When I lived in Alaska, a volcano erupted across Cook Inlet and sent a cloud of gray ash out over the water toward Anchorage. It was at first beautiful to watch as it made its way through a late-summer sunset to settle over the city. But then it overcame us, raining down ash like fine shards of glass to cover, coat, muddy, and ruin everything. This was a fairly mild eruption and fairly far away, with a body of water between the volcano and city. Yet Anchorage was shut down for several days as the ash damaged car engines and made breathing difficult.

Sin is a powerful force too. It can boil and brew beneath the surface of things until it erupts to consume with fiery yet somehow captivating devastation. The ashes we receive on Ash Wednesday remind me a bit of that volcanic cloud, beautiful, even alluring, until it comes to settle on me, overtaking me, marking me the sinner, working its way into my clothes and hair and skin and lungs and life in dangerous, corrosive ways.

After that volcanic eruption, as time passed and the rain came and people swept up and hosed off, Anchorage and the surrounding area were restored to the lush green that is usually Alaska just as fall descends. And I can't help but think that the life of faith is a bit like that too. We have our Ash Wednesdays, our seasons of Lent, our periods of shut down from the fallout of sin, but given a little grace, a little time, and a little help from heaven, even the most ruinous life can be restored to fertile beauty. "Remember that you are dust, and unto dust you shall return" has a most merciful companion phrase: "Remember that the reign of Easter has come to wash all the ash away."

45

THE SIXTH STATION:
VERONICA WIPES THE FACE OF JESUS

....

WHEN I WAS IN HIGH SCHOOL, I had the opportunity
to work as a page on the House floor of the U.S.
Congress in Washington, D.C. It was an extraordinary
experience to see the inner workings of our government,
meet other pages and congresspeople from every area of
the country, and stand on the House floor while Geraldine
Ferraro gave her acceptance speech as the first woman to
vie for the vice presidency. It was also quite cool to get my
hand on C-SPAN dropping a bill in the hopper. Sadly, and
probably true to my self-obsessed teenage inclinations, I
do not remember the bill or its significance, only that my
hand was on television. Oh, to have famous fingers.

There were other benefits to living on Capitol Hill,
namely, the Smithsonian and the National Gallery. I spent
every free minute I had wandering through the art gal-
leries, and I was particularly captivated by one painting:
The Veil of Veronica (c. 1615), by Domenico Fetti. I visited

it often and bought the print for two dollars in the gallery bookstore and brought it home with me. I still have it underneath a huge coffee-table book on impressionism that sits in my living room. I take it out from time to time, particularly during the Lenten season.

Later on, I learned the historical and artistic significance behind the painting, why it was that it was worthy of hanging in the National Gallery. Fetti is said to have studied Rubens and Caravaggio, among others, and the influence of the Venetian painters is evident in his work. A heightened awareness of and reverence for relics during his day probably influenced Fetti and his selection of topic. It was about that time in Rome that the relic of Veronica's veil was installed at St. Peter's Basilica. According to tradition, a woman stepped forward during Christ's way to the cross and offered her kerchief so that he might wipe his brow. When Christ returned the kerchief to the woman, the image of his face had miraculously been imprinted on the cloth. The Latin phrase for "true image," *vera icon,* over time was assigned to the woman who stepped forward, Veronica.

Whether any of this actually happened was of no significance to me as a teenager (and still isn't). At the time, I only knew that I was drawn to the image on the cloth, the sorrowful and holy face of Christ—the painting of a painting, in some respects. It captured this holy moment when two of God's precious creatures reached for each other, hoping for comfort, connection, some small measure of human relief. I wondered, *Would it have been more painful to be the one on the way to crucifixion, or to watch the one you love on the way?* My young heart ached at the injustice of having to occupy either position. There had to be relief. I couldn't believe in God if there was no answer to this suffering. I wanted to understand this Jesus and this Veronica. The ambitious and demanding emotions and thoughts of a young person aching for discovery swept through me. I longed for a universe that made sense. How could this impossible painting offer order to my world? Life seemed somehow easier in the impressionist wing; still I longed for resolution.

Who were they in this moment? What brought them to this pained point? Why would Jesus allow his image to remain with her in this way? Who was Veronica to him? What kind of love gives you the strength to watch your beloved suffer? Could I, would I ever love like that? Did I even want to?

Scripture does not mention Veronica. The details of Veronica's story arose in the centuries following Christ's passion and death. Her story evolved as did the tradition of the stations of the cross and other devotions. I wonder if God allowed her story to flourish because it can teach us something about the power of simply taking action, of doing what we can. A woman steps forward from the crowd. She is surrounded by an angry mob, red faced and

jeering, their faces tight with rage. Maybe they were spit-
ting, or watching in dumb horror, or watching with con-
tempt and satisfaction.

And she steps out, a woman of little consequence to
her culture, so little that for centuries she didn't even have
a name. She's near Jesus, his face dripping with blood, with
sweat, with tears perhaps, stained and burning. She wipes
his face, or maybe just hands the cloth to Christ so he can
wipe his own brow. She does what she can. This tiny comfort, this whisper of kind relief, of care. How powerful.

It is the most precious and tender thing there is, the
greatness of our care for one another: Christ willing to give
his life, Veronica willing to step forward and offer relief.
Their offerings seem hopelessly mismatched. But you
would not think it to examine Christ's face in that canvas.
God is not out to measure the greatness of our actions in
the same way we do. I think instead he is interested in
the motivation of our hearts, the kind of measuring that
speaks to fullness and integrity of heart.

I want to step forward from the crowd. I want to possess those gentle hands and a heart moved to action, even
simple action. I want the kind of heart that is willing to
go the distance, to stand and offer what little I have, what
minor relief I can provide if it's all I have at the point of
greatest suffering, and not shrink away. God will not reject
me if I flee, if I run away as Peter did, and I have run away
and probably will again. But I want to be Veronica, and I

know God sees this and is increasing this desire in me. He did it for Veronica. He will for me too. And I trust he will also leave behind his image, his true image, enmeshed like paint on the cloth of my very heart.

With love for Mary M.

46

The Tenth Station:
Jesus Is Stripped of His Garments

M Y FAVORITE VERSION OF this station from the stations of the cross hangs in St. Clement Eucharistic Shrine in Boston. The stations there are carved wooden reliefs and have been painted by the brother of one of the priests of the Oblates of the Virgin Mary, a very talented artist. His depiction of Christ being stripped of his garments, with its sorrowful shades and muted colors, is especially moving to me. His artwork captures so beautifully the final laying bare of Jesus, the last humiliating step before his crucifixion, the last debasing weight before his inevitable and gruesome death. It is a scene worthy of prolonged meditation, and it captures one of the gentlest, yet most intricate and telling aspects of our Savior. When I'm wondering whether a situation is designed for my humility or my humiliation, I go to the tenth station.

Though this scene is barely alluded to in Scripture, we can safely assume that before he was crucified, Jesus was stripped of his clothing. Later, soldiers would cast lots for the bloody tunic. The passage that describes this is a fulfillment of the prophetic Scripture in the Psalms: "They divide my clothes among themselves, and for my clothing they cast lots" (John 19:24; see Psalm 22:18).

God certainly knows the difference between humility and humiliation; this is a critical distinction I must make as well if I want to grow closer to the heart of God. Jesus was gentle with sinners who needed it, such as Mary Magdalene, meeting them in their most tender and exposed moments with healing acceptance and love. He was forthright and forceful with others, such as the Pharisees, whose hearts were hardened and full of self-righteous indignation. To all, he spoke the truth.

In his mercy, God corrects, disciplines, and edifies, and he knows to what degree and in what perfect way his children need correction and humbling. However, I cannot believe that God is interested in humiliating his children. Those who would say he is have not met the Jesus I am coming to know and may be missing the important purpose of humility.

In psychological terms, we might think of the difference between humility and humiliation as the difference between healthy and unhealthy shame.

Shame is God given; it is a necessary barometer that indicates to us when we've done something wrong. We don't naturally blush without a reason. Our faces flush in moments of shame because our bodies were designed in many ways to reflect the condition of our spirit. In a moment of shame, we want to cover up, to hide. We need shame in order to develop healthy boundaries as his beloved children and to know when we have crossed a boundary and wrongly damaged others or ourselves. We might feel ashamed in such a moment, but as uncomfortable as that feeling might be, it would be far worse to go without that interior correction.

When I was a kid of about five, I dived into a lake immediately behind a motorboat when its motor was running. I was an excellent swimmer even at that age and didn't think a thing of it, but when I came up to the surface, my father was screaming at me to get out of the water. I felt incredibly embarrassed and ashamed, until later, when I realized what could have become of me had my young limbs been caught up in the blades of the motor. I still remember how bad it felt to have my father yelling at me that way, and I never, ever jumped in the water behind a running motorboat again.

In the same way, the instruction of God is precious and merciful and life-giving! "How happy is the one whom God reproves; therefore do not despise the discipline of the Almighty. For he wounds, but he binds up; he strikes, but his hands heal" (Job 5:17–18). God-given shame never comes alone; it is always accompanied by God's healing. Humility in this sense helps us see ourselves honestly and in the right perspective. When humility results from loving correction, thank your lucky stars; you're being protected.

When we feel inappropriately ashamed, however, something evil may be at work.

When we are stripped raw and inappropriately exposed as Jesus is in the tenth station—be it in our bodies, our hearts, or our minds—it is designed to humiliate and crush us. Where healthy shame comes from God and lets us know when we've crossed a boundary or done something wrong or dangerous, unhealthy shame causes us to question our value as human beings, even our right to live. It suggests not that we've done something wrong, but that we are something wrong. Believing that we are worthless can keep us from growing closer to Jesus, and Satan knows this very well. It is one of his most insidious and damaging weapons against us.

But God is merciful; we don't have to take up that wrong belief. We can go to the tenth station. What the soldiers intended as humiliation for Jesus, he bore and accepted in humility. In doing so, he helps us bear up under the humiliation that others may try to cast upon us for our choices, faith, convictions, or love of God. In fulfilling that prophetic passage of Scripture, Jesus made it possible for us to discern the difference between humility and humiliation, and taught us too that humiliation does not get the final word. No matter how bad humiliation feels in the moment, resurrection is on the way.

People or circumstances may cause you to question your worth. That's all right. Just remember that God humbles; he never humiliates. God instructs us in right and wrong so that we might live more freely. We can trust that what God wishes to strip from us is not our dignity, but rather anything keeping us from being close to him. He is our ultimate source of humility and our only means of being stripped of damaging attitudes and behaviors. I go to the tenth station when I am trying to let go of something that keeps me from being close to God: fear, pride, resentment, self-pity, selfishness, unhealthy shame. Here I ask God to remove the obstacle from me, to correct any wrong beliefs, and to keep me humble and completely dependent on him.

Is God capable of stripping away all that would keep me far from him? Absolutely. But he will do so without stripping me of my worth, without leaving my wounds raw and exposed. He is ultimately my Comforter, my Healer, and if I let him come in and correct and heal and comfort, nothing can keep me from his great love, and there is no humiliation there.

Jesus, strip me of all the fear and weakness that binds me to myself. In your mercy, free me. Remove everything that is keeping me from being close to you.

47

The Hour of Divine Mercy

....

So it's three o'clock in the afternoon. Maybe you're sitting in your office, or changing a baby's diaper, or paying your bills, or watching a football game. Maybe it's an ordinary day. Maybe you're on a plane or at basketball practice or picking your kids up from school. It's three o'clock. So what?

In her diaries, St. Faustina described 3:00 PM as "the moment mercy was opened wide for every soul" and as "the hour of grace for the whole world. " (*Diaries of St. Faustina*, 1572).

Every soul, she said. *The whole world.* That's a lot of grace for sixty short minutes.

Of course, there is no magic in the hour, but there is power in the remembering that we do in that hour. In the three o'clock hour, many Catholics recall the death of Jesus on the cross and cast a little prayer heavenward in honor of his passion.

Jesus, I trust in you.

Jesus, mercy.

Jesus.

Catholics honor many little traditions that anchor us not so much in this world, but oh-so-solidly in "the next." It's one of the things I love most about being Catholic: the constant realization that I am living not just in this temporal world, this country, this state, this city, but I am, right now, living in eternity too. The traditions surrounding the Hour of Divine Mercy are meaningful reminders that, yes, I do live in an eternal continuum. This hour calls me also at times to ask the question, am I living *for* eternity?

The recognition of the Hour of Divine Mercy began with a simple, humble sister who has since been canonized: St. Faustina. Born in Poland in 1905, Mary Faustina Kowalska was poor and uneducated, the third of ten children. She entered the Congregation of the Sisters of Our Lady of Mercy at age twenty. After a life of great suffering, she died at age thirty-three.

Though simple and hidden from much of the world, St. Faustina's life was blessed with many supernatural experiences, including visions, revelations, and prophecies. At the direct request of her superiors (and Jesus, who spoke to her during visions), St. Faustina kept detailed diaries. They are powerful, vulnerable recordings of an extraordinary relationship between Jesus and one of his most precious and devoted daughters. They have now been translated into many languages.

St. Faustina was given a unique calling to spread the message of God's mercy. According to her diaries, she was specifically requested to record her revelations "for the benefit of those who by reading these things will be comforted in their souls and will have the courage to approach [Jesus]." Straight to the softened and waiting heart of this gentle, quiet saint, God expressed his deepest and most loving longing: "I do not want to punish aching mankind, but I desire to heal it, pressing it to My Merciful Heart" (1588).

This is the Jesus whom I have come to know, not just during the Hour of Divine Mercy, but truly at every hour—the Jesus who desires to heal my aching heart. This is the Jesus who waits for me in the tabernacle, in the Eucharist, in all the sacraments, and at adoration. This is the Jesus whom I call upon at three o'clock in the afternoon, through the merit of his holy wounds, his passion, and his death. *Jesus, mercy, I trust in you.*

Jesus' request to St. Faustina that we remember him at the Hour of Divine Mercy is certainly not the only example of Jesus asking us specifically to remember something. At the Last Supper, when Jesus instituted the sacrament of Holy Communion, he also invoked our remembering: "Do this in remembrance of me." It wasn't some vain request or bid for fame; it was an invitation to remember and accept his mercy, his grace, his forgiveness, his love. In her diaries, St. Faustina records that Jesus requested specifically that we recall his passion at the three o'clock hour. He promised great graces to those who honored the hour: "I will refuse nothing to the soul that makes a request of me in virtue of my passion" (1320).

Sometimes, Catholics are misunderstood because of our penchant to recognize and celebrate so many saints, feast days, moments of significance, holy places, and holy objects. We might look a little superstitious to people outside the faith tradition. The Hour of Divine Mercy may look like the Catholic version of glass slippers: click your heels three times while chanting "There's no place like heaven," and watch the graces pour down upon you. But that's missing the point. It's not about magic; it's about remembering and drawing on the rich, abundant experience that is the life of faith and the Mystical Body of Christ, the eternal continuum we all share.

I started this chapter on September 11. That date will always bring to my mind crashing towers, horrific loss of life, bitter grieving, shock, and the unimaginable depths of hatred necessary to facilitate such gruesome acts of terrorism. There is no magic in the date September 11, just as there's no magic in the three o'clock hour, but there is power and meaning and energy in the remembering. The question is, how do I want to direct that power and energy and meaning? Do I direct it in thanksgiving, in loving memory, in adoration and supplication? Or do I let it simply pass me by as I type away or answer the doorbell or wash the dishes or teach a class? As a country, we don't want to forget 9/11. As a Catholic, I don't want to forget the three o'clock hour.

Most of us are not going to be given a mission as dramatic as that of St. Faustina. I for one am rather relieved at the mercy of that! However, I can celebrate the mystery of God's mercy and the extraordinary gifts of insight he offered to us through this precious daughter of his at every three o'clock hour. I can join with the communion of saints awash in the eternal mercy of heaven and thank my Jesus that "mercy triumphed over justice" (1572).

Next time your clock strikes 3:00 PM, send a prayer heavenward, thank God for his mercy, and celebrate the blessings of mercy and love that unfold.

My Jesus, I trust in you.

48

TENEBRAE

....

God is in the darkness.
—Rainer Maria Rilke

O F THE MANY POIGNANT SERVICES celebrated within
the church, few are so moving to me as Tenebrae.
Taken from the medieval Latin, *tenebrae* means "darkness"
or "shadows." Tenebrae services are usually celebrated on
the Wednesday, Thursday, and Friday of Holy Week and
are a deeply symbolic way to enter into the solemnity
of Christ's passion and death. Through the chanting of
Scripture accompanied by the gradual darkening of the
church, participants revisit the darkness and shadow that
fell upon the face of the earth when Jesus was condemned,
crucified, and buried.

There are many rich variations of Tenebrae, but in a
traditional service, all enter a dimly lit church in silence.
On the altar, a Tenebrae hearse (something like a candela-
bra) holds a number of lit candles. After a priest leads the
opening prayer, the congregation (or some combination of
congregation, cantor, and choir) chants readings from the

Psalms and Lamentations. Following each reading, one of the candles in the hearse is extinguished, until finally the church is left in darkness. After a period of prolonged silence, a loud, rumbling note from an organ or another instrument symbolizes the earthquake or disquiet of nature at the moment of Christ's death. In some services, the last candle burning, meant to represent Christ as light of the world, is hidden behind the altar as a symbol of the three days he spent in the tomb. In a service following this practice, the rumbling noise following the period of silence may symbolize the earthquake at the moment of Christ's resurrection. The last light is then taken out of hiding and restored to its place on the altar, representing Christ's victory over death. All depart as they entered, in silence and dim light.

At the Last Supper, Christ asked us to "do this in remembrance of me." In Tenebrae, we are choosing to remember and reflect upon the deep sorrow, abandonment, and loneliness that Christ suffered during the Passion. Tenebrae readings or chants are cries to the heavens from a soul forgotten. "Save me, O God," cries the psalmist, "for the waters have come up to my neck. . . . I am weary with my crying; my throat is parched. My eyes grow dim with waiting for my God" (Psalm 69:1–3). The theme is continued through the weeping of the Lamentations: "How lonely sits the city that once was full of people! How like a widow she has become, she that was great among the nations! . . . She weeps bitterly in the night; . . . she has no one to comfort her; all her friends have dealt treacherously with her, they have become her enemies" (1:1–2).

Tenebrae is a concentrated reminder of how dark our existence can become outside the light of God. The sorrow, pain, abandonment, and loneliness of Christ during the Passion are the same sorrow, pain, abandonment, and loneliness we all feel when we are separated from God's love. No matter what circumstances or choices take us to dark places, we are reminded in Tenebrae that we are not alone; Christ has suffered these torments in as real and powerful a way as any of us. And the light of Christ, which could not be permanently extinguished but only momentarily contained in a tomb, is on its way to us in the darkest of places. The earth trembled and the skies cried out, and at the appointed time Christ was resurrected. Because of this, our "resurrection" to light is possible.

The spiritual life has moments of darkness. If it didn't, how would we recognize light or come to understand the difference between light and darkness? I once read that the opposite of faith is not doubt but certainty. If we don't have moments of darkness, do we really have faith, or do we just have certainty in our own conclusions? The real enemy of souls is not darkness that causes us to doubt God's love for us or that he has remembered us. The real enemy is the certainty that we can make it on our own. Sometimes, we have to go to dark places. Sometimes, we have to accept the darkness of the world, the sin of our choices and the choices of those around us, the darkness of our hearts.

While the last candle burns, the canticle of Zechariah is chanted: "Blessed be the Lord . . . for he has looked favorably on his people and redeemed them. . . . By the tender mercy of our God, the dawn from on high will break upon us, to give light to those who sit in darkness and in the shadow of death, to guide our feet into the way of peace" (Luke 1:68, 78–79).

Tenebrae is the dark reminder of our sin and of the perpetual compassion of our God, who will pierce that darkness and set us free.

49

EASTER

....

I F YOU LOOK UP THE definition of *resurrection,* you'll find synonyms such as *reawakening, resuscitation, rebirth.* Your dictionary might read "rising again after death," or "bringing back into use or memory." I will confess that it took me some years to grow into the belief that the resurrection of Jesus Christ was not some heavy-handed metaphor or moral tale. I could get pretty comfortable with the idea that faith in God, my "spiritual walk" through life, was a kind of metaphorical *reawakening, renewal,* or *rebirth* of sorts. Those words were easy enough to put on and walk around in, but after a very long while I realized that they just covered up my heart, like a coat. They didn't *live* there.

So it was back to this word, this heavy burden: *resurrection.*

It took some time and living and the sweetness of God's gift of faith for me to come to believe that Jesus

Christ—who had healed the sick, befriended outcasts, taught women, and said, "Let the children come"—was brutally crucified and buried for three days, and then got up and walked around the earth again. Truly. People saw him and spoke to him and ate with him; Thomas touched him. Many of these people were the same witnesses who saw Jesus crucified and helped bury his lifeless body.

It took me more time and greater graces to come into believing that this man born of woman, this Son of God, this Jesus, died for your sins and mine. The shedding of his innocent blood, the sacrifice of his life makes it possible for you and for me to enter divine life.

He rose again, not to enter into ordinary life and die later—as Lazarus did, for example—but so that he could enter into eternal life, a life beyond time and space, beyond death. Jesus promised that the power to lay down his life and take it up again was his and his alone. The Resurrection was a fulfillment of that ultimate promise of life-giving authority, and so I have courage and confidence to go to Jesus in all things, to trust all his promises, to embrace his whole teaching, his whole way of life, and to accept his forgiveness, grace, and love. Because I know that Jesus has authority over life and death, I am able to believe that I can rise again too.

Not long ago, I took a six-month class on the Spiritual Exercises of St. Ignatius of Loyola. Once a week, I met with a small group of others who were doing the daily meditations and we talked about our experiences with the rigor of Ignatian meditation. During Holy Week, the director asked us, "What does it mean to you that Christ died and rose again? What does that change for you on a daily basis?" There was no judgment or condescension in the question; it was posed earnestly, and I was earnestly stumped by it. It hovered plain and simple before me, and I was surprised to hear a great internal pause in my heart, followed by a quiet and curious "I don't know." I usually felt pretty confident in my answers, my opinions, and my thoughts. My fine mind had been well educated and well tested, hadn't it? I knew with certainty—didn't I?—about this resurrection business.

Still, there I sat, with the emptiness and humility of "I don't know."

It is a truly gifted place to be, a wonderful, powerful place, this position of unknowing, of not having the answer. It's one of the reasons I love true students: they're teachable. Those who come into the classroom and sit down with the attitude of "I don't know what you know. Will you show me what you know?" are truly humble creatures. They have come to that teetering edge where not knowing and knowing meet; they are ready to leap into the soft and tangled thicket of understanding. A student in that frame of mind is truly teachable and is far more likely to receive what he or she came to class for in the first place.

I believe that God rushes to meet us when we move even one finger into this vulnerable place of not knowing. When you come to God humbly with your earnest questions, look out!—your life will change. It may not become full of *answers,* but it will become full of *love.*

Answers I may never have, but faith has been given to me in abundance, multiplied by grace that I could not conjure for myself. And Jesus is not afraid of my lack of faith. God is big enough to handle my anger, resentment, and self-pity; my Father is not put off by my doubts and fears and questions. What stifles my relationship with him more often than anything else is my certainty.

Easter cannot exist for you and for me without a deep willingness to embrace the mystery of love at its most fundamental: he who was dead now lives; I who was lost am found. I don't ever pretend to understand that. Even that willingness is a gift. I could tell you that I am certain that Jesus rose from the dead, but it is far more accurate to say that I *believe* that he did, and because he did, I have a perpetual invitation into divine life. His death paid for my sin; his Resurrection opened the door for me to new life. *New life.* I believe it. I live it.

Certainty requires proof, but faith requires love above all else. Certainty resides solely in the mind, but belief resides in the mind and heart. Certainty lives on intellect alone, but belief lives through a greater commitment, a greater sacrifice—it lives through my flesh-and-blood heart.

I could bring my mind to the Resurrection—and certainly, I do; faith and reason are not opposed to each other.

But resurrection means nothing if I check my heart at the door.

In the Crucifixion, in the Mass, my sweet and gentle Jesus lays his heart out on the altar; in love, he conserves himself not one bit but pours himself out entirely—for you, for me, for all of us, now and forever. But then, the stone rolls away and the light spills in, and angels appear and say, "He is risen." It's Easter.

I believe it.

Epilogue: The Cross

Life can be devastatingly cruel and full of disappointment. It is perhaps no more piercing than when we are rejected. We flung the door to our hearts wide open to someone, and he or she didn't come in to make themselves at home. We admitted our most precious and vulnerable needs—to be wanted, to be desired, to be forgiven—and were met with the sting of disdain, betrayal, or, worse, indifference. We asked someone to love us, and he or she refused. Sometimes in honesty, sometimes in recklessness, sometimes in naïveté or selfishness, we bind ourselves again and again to the outcome of our loving. In order to love, we are dependent on love in return. That's not asking too much, we think. That's the way it's supposed to work, isn't it?

There is no other ache like that of potential lost, hopes shattered, dreams undone, love abandoned. It bruises right down to the bone.

I used to think that the cross was a bitter pill just like rejection. I had to choke it down with blind acceptance, or all heavenly bets were off. If I didn't swallow it up, a perpetual mocking mantra of "There's no room at the inn" awaited me, and that was all there was to it.

Thank you, Sweet Jesus, I don't believe that anymore.

Still, there it is—arms outstretched in agony; nails piercing flesh and bone; blood and bitter gall; a weight of innocence and weariness too great to measure; cruel thorns; taunting, humiliating, soul-piercing rejection.

What difference did any of it make? It was two thousand years ago, on a continent I will likely never set foot upon, in a time that bears little resemblance to my own— at least on the surface. What possible difference could it make to me, walking around in my little world?

Christ's suffering has to count for something, but what?

Sometimes I think I place too much emphasis on trying to understand a thing rather than trying to accept it. I want to wrap the mysteries of the Almighty, the Creator, the Holy One into nice, neat little packages I can carry around in my purse and take out when feeling doubtful, insecure, afraid. Like a perfume I can dab at my pulse points, "the essence of forgiveness." I want the fullness of the transubstantiation in twenty words or less, or "the dummy's guide to grace." I want something tangible, something that makes sense.

But the cruelty of the cross is senseless, as is all cruelty—incomprehensible, almost too much to believe. And the list of modern flavors of cruelty mirrors those of ages past and is only growing longer and perhaps more sophisticated and insidious. Most of us have tasted our fair share. But keeping a running tab of our injuries is surely not the point either and, at the very least, is not useful.

The aspect of the cross that stops me short is that, throughout his passion and death, Christ was himself. He never tried to be anything else, never tried to please anyone, never tried to run away, never wavered from the truth; he only occupied himself completely and authentically with his own calling. He just loved, no matter the outcome; just loved, because that is what he was created to do. The miracle of the cross is that God loves anyway, no matter the result, no matter our choice, no matter the flighty vacillations of the sometimes fickle human heart—loving one minute, resenting the next, indifferent or self-involved in still the next. Instead, he flings the door to his very sacred saving heart wide, wide, and invites all to enter and make themselves at home. Ultimately, there is only one reason for me to be Catholic: the cross. At every Mass, in every sacrament, in every spiritual discipline, in these ways and innumerably more, we are invited to the cross, that wide-flung door.

Christ's suffering counts for something, the most important things, essential things. It counts for grace and for mercy. It counts for authenticity and for resurrection from our ruination and into who we truly are: children of light. It counts for being genuine and honest. It counts for love.

As my faith grows up within me, more and more the prayer I once clung to, "God, remove my pain," becomes

"If I must experience this suffering, then please, let it count for something. Just don't let it go to waste." When I can open my heart and love anyway, no matter the outcome, no matter the choices of people around me, no matter the risk involved, I become more powerful in heaven's kingdom than any army, any fear, any cruelty, or any rejection. Instead, those things are swallowed up whole and lost in grace and mercy. I find that when they are awash in love, they're not such bitter pills after all.

I want to love anyway, to love because that's what I was created to do. And I can trust that God will never let any potential resulting suffering go to waste if I'm doing that. It will always count, and that's a promise. Even when I don't know it; even when I can't feel it. And that gives me courage, courage to love again, to love anyway.

I don't understand the cross. I don't believe understanding it is the point, or even necessarily a very worthy or interesting goal. But I think accepting it is—accepting that we were created to love no matter the outcome. The cross is God's promise to love us, no matter what. And deep in my spirit where the most essential parts of me are anchored, there is a knowing, growing and resonant and burning with an eternal ache that tells me: the cross counts. It matters. It counts for grace and mercy. It counts for love.

Also by Liz Kelly . . .

The Rosary
A Path into Prayer

ISBN 0-8294-2024-X • 5" x 7" Pb • 216 pp • $11.95

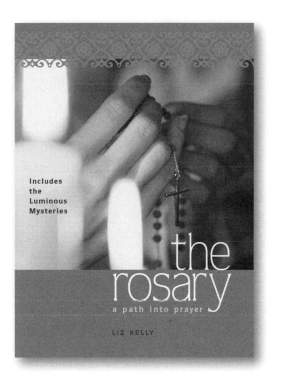

The Rosary, an updated and revised version of
The Seeker's Guide to the Rosary (Loyola Press),
is a comprehensive look at the history, practice,
and benefits of rosary devotion. Now includes
the Luminous Mysteries.

Join In. Speak Up. Help Out!

....

LOYOLA PRESS INVITES YOU TO become one of our Loyola Press Advisors! Join our unique online community of people willing to share with us their thoughts and ideas about Catholic life and faith. By sharing your perspective, you will help us improve our books and serve the greater Catholic community.

From time to time, registered advisors are invited to participate in online surveys and discussion groups. Most surveys will take less than ten minutes to complete. Loyola Press will recognize your time and efforts with gift certificates and prizes. Your personal information will be held in strict confidence. Your participation will be for research purposes only, and at no time will we try to sell you anything.

Please consider this opportunity to help Loyola Press improve our products and better serve you and the Catholic community. To learn more or to join, visit **www.SpiritedTalk.org** and register today.

—The Loyola Press Advisory Team